A Place to Warm Your Heart

A Trilogy of Hope and Inspirational Poems

By

Linda C. Luebke

I

A Place to Warm Your Heart
A Trilogy of Hope and Inspirational Poems

Published by: Linda C. Luebke
16019 Swallow Street NW
Andover, MN 55304

ISBN: 0-9705105-1-9

Printed in the United Stated of America by

Morris Publishing
3212 East Highway 30
Kearney, NE 68847
800-650-7888

Dedication

With a great deal of gratitude I dedicate
this book to my husband, Allen M. Luebke.
I appreciate all of the love and support he has given
to me throughout the past thirty-five years.
His extraordinary gift of love and respect
remains my inspiration.

I also wish to dedicate this book to my parents,
Barbara and Orville Krotzer who taught
me the value of faith, hope, and love.
I love you.

Acknowledgments

First and foremost I want to thank God for the gift of His love, as well as the gift of the Song Poems and stories in this book. I pray Jesus will be with everyone who reads them, and give each of you a special blessing.

I want to thank those of you who allowed me to use the events in your lives to tell the stories contained within this book. I recognize the sacrifice each of you made by having to revisit these difficult times in your lives, and I thank you for your willingness to open old wounds in an effort to show others there is always hope. Thank you.

I wish to thank Ann L. Johnson for all of her help with the mechanics of this book. She worked tirelessly finding my many errors and mistakes. She is a gracious and beautiful person and I have been privileged to know her in this life. Thank you so very much Ann.

I want to thank Ginny Jorgenson and Myrna Chipman for their help with this book. They read and reread my manuscript in an effort to find my many errors. I appreciate all of their help and support.

I offer a special thank you to my friends and family for all of your love and support during this project. I appreciate the encouragement and help you gave to me.

The stories in this book are inspired by actual events although names, dates, locations and specifics have been changed or fictionalized in an effort to insure the anonymity of the people involved as per their request. Any similarity to any person or persons not connected to this project is purely coincidental.

Table of Contents

- **Listen With Your Heart**.....Inspirational Poem 1

- **In Search of Destiny**.....Inspirational Story.....2

- **Lord Rest My Soul**..... Inspirational Poem.....21

- **A Better Man**..... Inspirational Poem.....22

- **Have You Heard**..... Inspirational Poem.....23

- **The Garden**.....Inspirational Story.....24

- **With Grace and Tender Mercies**..... Poem.....60

- **Hope Lives On**..... Inspirational Poem.....61

- **With Nothing Less Than Love**..... Poem.....62

- **If seeing Is Believing**..... Inspirational Poem.....64

- **Not Just on Christmas Morning**..... Poem.....65

- **If I Should Fall**.......... Inspirational Poem.....67

- **Through the Darkest Night**..... Inspirational Story.....68

- **Have Faith**..... Inspirational Poem.....104

- **With Nothing More Than Everything**..... Poem.....105

- **With Passing Time**..... Inspirational Poem.....106

- **Come Walk With Me**..... Inspirational Poem.....107

Introduction

If you are among those who read my first book, you probably think you know what to expect in this one. Surprise! To be completely honest with you the pages contained within are not what I expected to write.

Strange thing about life, how it seems to move us into areas we never thought we'd go. When I sat down to write this book, I fully expected it to take a completely different path. When this book began to take the twists and turns it did, I seriously questioned my ability to write this at all. But as always I prayed and asked for guidance, and then went back to work.

Taking a leap of faith, I jumped into this project with both feet and before I knew it, **A Place to Warm Your Heart** *A Trilogy of Hope and Inspirational Poems* was born. From the very beginning it took on a life of it's own and I held on for the ride. As with a wing and a prayer, I traveled down this uncharted course.

As I began to tell the stories sent to me by people wishing to share them, I found myself walking in their shoes, so to speak. I felt much of what they felt when placed in the life experiences each of them faced. To say this was very difficult and heart wrenching would be a major understatement. Somehow, I found my way through it and now I am passing their stories along to you.

I have read in my Bible, and know that Jesus often taught in parables. I believe He is trying to tell us something through the stories I have included, or perhaps I should say felt compelled to include, in this book. Every one of you may well get a different lesson from these stories and poems, but I believe Jesus will be with each of you when you read the book. If you ask Him to be with and teach you, He will give you what He wants you to take from *A Trilogy of Hope and Inspirational Poems.*

I will readily admit none of the topics addressed within these pages are what I thought the book would entail at its inception. But as with many things in life, when I will allow Jesus to lead the way my journey takes me to places I never thought I would go.

Now I invite you to join me as we walk through *A Trilogy of Hope and Inspirational Poems.* Take from it what you will, and I pray each of you will find a restful place within these pages.

Linda C. Luebke

A Place to Warm Your Heart

A Trilogy of Hope and Inspirational Poems

By

Linda C. Luebke

If we learn to listen with our hearts, Jesus will speak to us with compassion, love, grace, and forgiveness. He will hold us through the darkest of nights and shelter us from the storms of life. He is the peace we seek, the help we need, and all that is honest, right, and good. We need only to believe, and in faith reach out to Jesus. He will be beside us today, and throughout eternity. We need only to ask and believe.

Listen With Your Heart

Sometimes they may say something
They don't really mean to say.
Wanting to feel close to someone,
They might push you away.
It may not be the words you hear are eloquent end from start.
Your ears can't always hear the truth.
So, you must listen with your heart.

Afraid they might be turned from,
Or ashamed of what they've done,
They think that striking out
Is how the battle will be won.
Desperate to find their way, sometimes they may cry out in pain.
Are you listening with your heart
To what their words may not be saying?

Should they push you away,
When holding on is what they want to do?
With kindness and compassion,
Jesus can help them to get through.
Hold them in your heart drawing them into God's loving embrace.
With love, you can lead them
To seek a better place.

So, if in anger they strike out,
Or from fear the tears may fall.
If they would reach out with a prayer
God will help them through it all.
There's no mountain so high with God's help we can not climb
Armed with faith and love,
God will hold us for all time...

In Search of Destiny

Sharon was in the beginning of her sophomore year in high school and had a great deal to look forward to. At fourteen she was younger than most of the students in her class because she had jumped ahead a grade in elementary school, so she worked harder than most to try to fit in socially. She had just been accepted on the varsity cheerleading squad, and tonight would be her first game.

She was a pretty girl by anyone's definition with long dark hair, big brown eyes, and a very warming smile and gentle, giving nature. She came from a good family and lived in the better part of town in an upper middle class neighborhood. Sharon was a good student and was involved in most of the school activities.

Her father was in real estate and wasn't home much. He was very much involved in his career, and he was extremely goal oriented; making money was his primary goal. He was always so busy with work there was little time left for anything else in his life. Whereas he was a good provider, he found it difficult to show his love for his family other than in a financial way. Sharon knew he loved her, but he just never said it.

Her mother stayed home taking care of the house and raising Sharon and her older brother, Bobby. Sharon was very close to her mother, as was Bobby. Neither of them, however, was very close to their father.

Bobby was in his second year of college and had lived away from home for more than a year now. Sharon and Bobby had always been close, and it had been a long year for both of them having to get used to living without the other around for support. They spoke on the phone often and looked forward to the holidays when Bobby would come home from school.

At the game that night while Sharon was cheerleading with the rest of the squad, she noticed one of the players on the football team looking at her and smiling. She had seen him around school and knew him by name, but until now she hadn't really noticed him showing any interest in her. His name was John, and he was a very handsome senior. He was also a very talented painter. She had seen some of his paintings displayed around town. John was a good student and wanted to go to college, but was unable to do so for financial reasons. His family struggled to make ends meet because his father died when he was about seven, and his mother had to support the family on her own. John worked nights to help her and to be able to afford a car. His life style was very different from that of Sharon and her family.

They lived in a small town where everybody pretty much knew everybody. She had been aware of who John was for years and even thought her brother, Bobby, and he were friends, but until now, he was just one of the older guys in town. Sharon always thought he was cute but never entertained the idea that he might be interested in her.

After the game, everyone went out for a burger at the local burger shop where again, Sharon noticed John looking at her. When John walked over and offered to drive Sharon home, she was thrilled and tried hard not to show her excitement while accepting his offer. That was how they met. From that night on, a relationship grew that would ultimately change the course of both of their lives. They began dating and became high school sweethearts. Throughout that school year they were inseparable. When Sharon turned fifteen in February of that year, John gave her his class ring along with a promise of his love. She had his class ring and his heart, and she knew the feelings they had for one another were very special.

Sharon's mother liked John. She knew he was older than Sharon, but he was a decent person and she could see how much he cared for Sharon. Sharon's father didn't like him at all. He felt John would go nowhere in life and wasn't worthy of Sharon or her place in society. This caused a great deal of tension in the family, but I would suppose most families go through many of these same things.

As graduation drew ever closer for John, so did reality. Back in those years, all men had to register for the draft and they were expected to serve in the military. There was a war rearing its ugly head in a place far away named Vietnam. After graduation, John enlisted in the United States Army recognizing he had an obligation to fulfill. He also knew Sharon still had two years of high school to complete. He believed by getting his military service out of the way while Sharon was finishing high school, they could marry after both completed their obligations, and they could get on with their lives. Going into the Army wasn't something John really wanted to do, but he knew he had to do it sooner or later, and he saw no reason to put it off.

Before John went into the Army, Sharon bought a gold charm shaped like a heart that separated into two sections. Each section looked like a heart torn in two but when placed together made one whole heart. On the back of the charm she had the words inscribed: *One Heart Forever Joined With Love.* She bought two chains and placed one section of the heart on each chain, one for John to wear, and the other for herself. They both promised to wear them until they could be joined together again. This would be something John could take with him, and Sharon felt he could hold onto it when he felt lonely. She told him it would be like taking part of her with him.

When John left for boot camp, both Sharon and he felt the weight of the separation. She wrote to him every day, and he wrote as often as he could. She treasured his letters. When he finally finished his training and returned home on leave, they both knew theirs was a lifetime commitment. John bought Sharon a diamond ring, and they became secretly engaged. Recognizing that Sharon was very young, John believed her father would put less pressure on her if he didn't know about the engagement for a while. He believed this would make her life easier in general during his absence. They did tell both of their mothers, swearing them to secrecy, and of course they told Bobby too.

Until now, Sharon and John had decided to wait until they were married to share the more physical aspects of an intimate relationship between a man and a woman. They both expected and intended to wait. But two days before he was to return to the base, realizing he may well be shipped over to Vietnam, their best intentions gave way to the passion of the moment, and Sharon and John crossed the threshold they both promised not to cross. They spent the last two days of his leave together making memories they could both hold onto until they could be together again. If John was sent overseas, they knew they would be separated for a year, or possibly more, and the time they had to spend together now took on new meaning for both of them.

When John had to leave for the base two days later, they were both glad they hadn't waited. At that point in their lives, they had made a lifetime commitment to one another, and neither of them felt any regret or guilt in having done so. As they said goodbye to one another while in an embrace, they prayed together asking God to bond them for life. They also asked God to be with John as he walked into the unknown.

John was shipped out to Vietnam less than a week later, and he called to say he loved Sharon with all his heart and soul just before he left. Promising to write as often as possible, the young lovers said goodbye. This was very difficult for both John and Sharon.

Sharon wrote and sent letters to John through the base as he instructed unsure of exactly when the letters would catch up with him, but knowing he would cherish every word when they did. Days turned to weeks and the weeks into months as she continued to send letters, hearing nothing from him, and not knowing if he was receiving her letters either. Listening to the accounts of the ongoing war on the television were the only connection Sharon could find to John now. This was extremely difficult and lonely for her as she waited to hear something from him. She missed him terribly and worried about him. She prayed asking Jesus to keep him safe. At this point, all she could do was wait.

During the next two and a half months, Sharon began to feel ill. The stress of waiting to know that John was all right was taking a toll on this young woman, but she began to suspect something more was going on as well. As the pressure of the situation moved her closer to the breaking point, Sharon needed to talk to someone. Bobby was away at college and she was feeling more isolated and alone with every passing day.

Staying home from school one morning with flu symptoms, she confided to her mother that she thought she might be pregnant. Her mother made an appointment for her and later that day took Sharon into the clinic. Within a few days Sharon knew for certain that she was pregnant after her family physician confirmed it. Having very mixed feelings about her situation, Sharon was both elated with the prospect of having John's child and fearful of what her father would say or do.

Sharon wrote another letter to John telling him he was going to be a father. She was sure he would want to know about the pregnancy as soon as possible, and she prayed this letter would reach him quickly. She knew John would help her through everything she would have to face, and she was wishing he were with her now. Sharon decided not to tell her father about the baby until she heard from John. Now holding on even more tightly to the engagement ring John had given her, she waited. The ring meant a great deal to her because it signified the promise of the lifetime commitment John had so willingly made to her.

She was sure she would hear something from him soon. Sharon knew John would be happy about the baby. Maybe this wasn't quite the way they planned for it to be, but she knew he would be happy. She also knew John would be a wonderful father. He often spoke about his father and remembered his dad with so much love. John often commented on how very much he missed him.

Four days after Sharon knew she was pregnant for certain, she received a visit form John's mother. She told Sharon she had just been informed that John had been killed in action about fifteen days after he arrived in Vietnam. With disbelief and shock, Sharon felt as if her world was coming to an end.

Sick with grief, now alone and pregnant, Sharon struggled to make sense of something that could make no sense. Pleading with God, begging Him to make this be a horrible mistake and let John be able to come home to her, she fought facing the inevitable with every ounce of strength she could muster within herself. This was so unfair. How could this happen? John never even knew he was going to be a father. He and Sharon didn't have enough time together, and now her heart was breaking beneath the weight of this loss.

How could things get any worse than this? At fifteen she would be at her father's mercy in regard to having and keeping this baby. Needing something to hold onto, the child she was carrying became everything to Sharon. She was determined to have and raise the child, alone if necessary.

Recognizing the baby was all she would have of John, and his child would be the only part of him she would be able to hold onto, the baby became her life. Sharon didn't know what to do. Her mother was willing to try to help her in any way she could, but her father was going to be another story. She prayed a lot over those next couple of days.

The funeral was unbearable for Sharon. Everyone in town was there. Bobby came home and was at her side, and that helped to keep her on an even keel, at least to some degree. All of John's friends came and a couple of his teachers stood up and spoke about what a wonderful young man had been taken and how very much he would be missed. During the service, Sharon sat next to John's mother at his mother's request, and she introduced Sharon as John's fiancée to her friends and family. Sharon was deeply touched by this.

Both of her parents attended the funeral. Her mother attended because she wanted to, and her father attended mainly because he thought it would look bad if he didn't. At one point as Sharon was introduced as John's fiancée, her father overheard it. The look on his face clearly told Sharon he wasn't happy. As if getting through the funeral wasn't bad enough, now she knew she would have to face the music with her father later as well.

Following John's funeral, she decided it was time to tell her father about the engagement and the baby and hope for the best. Before telling her father the whole truth, Sharon knew he would be angry at first, but she prayed after a little time he'd adjust to the idea. Her mother promised to help her in any way she could and Sharon decided to enlist the support of her older brother as well.

Bobby was very loving and supportive when he found out about his sister's circumstances and he offered her all of the support he could possibly give. He had known John for years before he started dating Sharon, and Bobby always liked him. Apparently before John left for Vietnam, he asked Bobby to watch over Sharon while he was gone. Of course Bobby said he would; he always had. Now he intended to keep that promise. So he insisted he be with her when she told their father.

With her mother and brother by her side for support, Sharon went to her father and told him everything. Expecting to see anger, she was surprised to see her father show some discomfort with the idea, but there was no big blow up as she had expected. Instead, he suggested that she go to stay with her aunt in another state to have the baby and give some thought to giving the child up for adoption since John wasn't going to be coming back home. He promised if she decided to keep the baby, he would help her to raise the child until she could make it on her own. He did insist, however, that she leave town for a while and also that she carefully considers all of her options.

Her father suggested they tell everyone she needed a break and was going to visit her favorite aunt for a while to help her get through the grieving process. He was afraid if people knew about the baby, the gossip about her situation might hurt his business, and he thought this was the best thing to do for all of them. In all honesty, Sharon expected much worse.

Sharon packed and went to stay with her Aunt Mary promising her father she would consider adoption. She tried, but deep in her soul she knew giving her baby up for adoption was something she couldn't do. This child was the only link to John she had left, and in her heart she was committed to both the baby and to John's memory. Sharon couldn't give the baby away under any circumstances.

Praying her father would understand, she finally told him that the baby would be coming home with her. She couldn't give up John's child for adoption. No, adoption was no longer being considered. Again, Sharon was surprised by her father's reaction to her decision when he simply said, "In that case we'll all have to make the best of it."

When Sharon went into labor two weeks early, both of her parents took a flight out to be with their daughter. Sharon knew her mother would come, but she was surprised to see her father. He'd never taken so much interest in her life before, or at least, he'd never shown quite so much interest outwardly. Although this seemed a bit out of character for him, his concern and support was a welcome relief to Sharon.

He told her he had some business in town anyway, so he could use the trip as a tax right-off. This was so typical of her father. Sharon had been through a lot, and she knew she needed all the help and support she could get, and whatever reason he chose to give for being there, the bottom line was, he was there.

After what appeared to be a normal labor and delivery, Sharon was handed her baby girl. She was beautiful and seemed to be perfectly healthy. As Sharon counted her little fingers and toes, she looked at the baby she knew John would have loved with all of his heart and soul, and she named their daughter Johnnie Marie. Sharon's mother held the baby and instantly fell in love with this perfect and perfectly beautiful human being, her first grandchild.

Sharon's father looked at the baby from a distance but seemed a little nervous about holding someone so tiny and said he'd take the plunge tomorrow. The baby was wrapped in a pretty pink receiving blanket and Sharon held her closely cherishing every moment she held her beautiful Johnnie Marie.

When one of the nurses came in to take Johnnie Marie back to the nursery for the night, Sharon didn't want to let her go. This was the first time she felt any real comfort and peace since John left her to go back to the base the last time they were together. But the nurse explained this was a hospital rule, and all the babies had to go back to the nursery at night. Sharon quickly changed Johnnie Marie and the nurse took her away for the night. Sharon had placed a different blanket around the baby after changing her and kept the pink one she had taken from around her baby. It smelled of her baby, you know the way all babies smell right after their bath, and this felt comforting to Sharon as she snuggled in for the night.

7

This had been a long day and Sharon was exhausted. Her parents left for the night and she went to sleep holding the pink receiving blanket close to her heart, wearing the engagement ring John had given her, and wearing her half of the heart charm necklace she had kept. She wondered if the other half of the charm would ever come back to her. It hadn't been returned with John's personal effects.

Sharon felt as if her heart had been ripped from her chest when John was killed, and this charm had almost become a symbol of that pain. Now with the birth of Johnnie Marie, she felt hope that the wound would someday heal. This was the first real peace Sharon had felt in months. She felt hope for the first time in a long time, and she knew this was a new beginning.

In the morning when she awoke, Sharon rang for the nurse and asked to have Johnnie Marie brought down to her. The nurse said someone would be down soon. Sharon's breakfast tray came, and she ate every bit of it realizing she had to keep her strength up for when she and Johnnie Marie could go home.

Again Sharon rang for the nurse and was told someone would be with her soon. Unwilling to wait another second, she walked down to the nursery and looked through the glass. Johnnie Marie's bed was empty, and Sharon began to insist someone give her the baby, now! Something was wrong; Sharon felt it.

The old doctor who had delivered Sharon's baby came out of an office and told her she should follow him. They went back to her room, and he asked her to sit down. Sharon didn't want to sit down and insisted she wanted to know where Johnnie Marie was.

The doctor told her that Johnnie Marie stopped breathing during the night and the staff was unable to revive her. He said there was nothing anyone could have done, and that these things just happen sometimes. He stated because the baby was somewhat premature, that may have been a contributing factor in her death, but they would never really know for sure.

Sharon sank to the floor in shock clutching the blanket her child had been wrapped in. Hearing her baby girl had died was more than she could handle, and Sharon collapsed. The doctor gave her a shot of something to help calm her, and the next few days were nothing more than a blur for Sharon. The next thing she actually could remember was being on a plane with her parents on her way home.

Johnnie Marie was gone and Sharon felt herself die inside. Holding to Johnnie Marie's pink blanket, Sharon began slipping further from her own sanity. Time passed and nothing helped to ease the pain she felt inside. The hope she had felt after the birth of her child had vanished into a cloud of pain that was smothering the life out of Sharon, and she didn't even care any more. Sharon felt as if everything that mattered to her had been taken away, and she had no reason to go on.

Back at home, her father told her she had to put all of this behind her and go on. She couldn't. She cried and grieved until there was nothing left, and when she was through, she only wanted to die. Sharon's mother took her to therapist after therapist but to no avail. Everyone tried to help her, but it was as if all hope was gone, and there was only emptiness left in its place. Time passed and Sharon stood still stuck in a haze of despair and misery that was crushing the life out of her.

Bobby had graduated from college and moved back close to home hoping to help his sister and to keep a promise he made to John. With nothing left to try, Bobby turned to God one night, and praying for his sister, he begged Jesus to help her. He asked for hope. He prayed for faith and strength. Then he got up from the chair where he had been sitting, and he went to get his sister. He knew he had to do something.

"Sharon, come with me," Bobby said as he took her hand and led her out of the house that had become a tomb for Sharon. She had shut herself off from everyone and everything around her. "Look at this," Bobby said, as he handed her a little puppy. "His name is Future. He's alone in this world and he needs someone to take care of him. I can't do it. I've got a new job and a new girlfriend who sneezes every time she gets too close to him. Can you help me out here?"

"Future? What kind of a name is that for a puppy? You've got to be kidding," Sharon stated, completely unaware of her brothers plan to bring her back to some kind of life.

"He's young, if you don't like his name, change it," retorted Bobby trying to get a reaction out of his sister. "Just keep one thing in mind. If you don't take Future, he ain't got one."

"That's terrible, Bobby. He's a helpless little creature who needs love just like everybody else," Sharon said as she picked the dog up and cuddled him. "You just need someone to love you, don't you, pal?" This was the first time Sharon made any connection to anything since she lost Johnnie Marie.

Bobby took a deep breath and with a prayer he told his sister he loved her and that she was right, everyone needs love. He explained how he had promised John that he would take care of her for him until he came back home, and he felt he had broken that promise.

"John wouldn't want this for you. Sharon, he loved you, and so do I. Please stop killing yourself. I don't know why God took John and Johnnie Marie from you, but at least they're together. They're both in a better place than this, and you have to accept it. If you curl up and die too, their lives will have served no purpose. John would hate this. Please, Sharon, I can't stand to see this anymore. You have so much to live for. Live for John. Live for Johnnie Marie. Live for me, Sharon, please," Bobby begged as tears ran down his face believing he was in a fight for his sister's life that he had to win. "In Jesus name, please Sharon, try," he whispered.

The love Sharon had for her brother made her see his need to help her, and she finally understood that she was hurting him by giving up on life and herself. Bobby was right. John would hate this. She was so blinded by grief that she lost sight of everything else, and now she was hurting someone she loved dearly. This was so wrong, and now she could see it.

Future started barking, and Sharon held him tight with one arm and placed the other around her brother needing to comfort him. "Don't cry Bobby, I'll take your dog," Sharon said, trying to console her brother. "Old Future here's going to be just fine. I promise."

This was the first step in the healing process for Sharon to be followed by many others. For the first time since the loss of both John and Johnnie Marie, she felt something other than pain. She saw how deeply her brother loved her and how destructive her behavior had been. She never meant to hurt Bobby, or anyone else for that matter, but she had. Now, after all this time she could see it was time to stop allowing the grief to pull her under and do what she knew John would want her to do. Stepping out on faith that Jesus would light her way, Sharon took the first step into making a future for herself.

That night, while alone in her room, Sharon got on her knees and asked Jesus to help her. She begged His forgiveness for losing sight of all the love He had given her throughout the years. Sharon thanked God for having the chance to have loved John at all. She recognized that Johnnie Marie was truly a gift from heaven, and although she held her in her arms for only a short time, this was a gift she would always be thankful for having. She knew she would always cherish the memory of her tiny treasure.

As Sharon prayed, she asked that one day, if God would permit such a thing, she might be able to hold her baby in her arms just one more time. She would be forever grateful if it would be the first thing she could do when she got to heaven. From deep within her soul, Sharon felt a real need to ask this one thing of Jesus. Praying she felt somehow, someway, Jesus would make this wish come true. She never got to say goodbye to her baby and her need to do so was so strong, it overwhelmed her soul with an ache that tortured her to the core. Finally, she understood that Jesus knew her pain and felt it with her, and she knew He would help her through this now. With that, Sharon promised Jesus, she would do her best to move on, and from that day on, she did.

For the next few years she finished her education and made every effort to move forward with her life. She worked hard to attain her degree and she became a teacher. When she was twenty-five she was offered a teaching position in the local high school, and she began her life's work. Sharon dedicated her life to working with and helping children. She loved teaching, and it became her life.

Over the years Sharon never stopped loving John. There was always a place in her heart that belonged to him. She had memories of the time they had together, and those memories were comforting to her. The little things she had saved from the prom or from the drive they took to the beach became treasures she could look back on. She had the love letters he wrote her from boot camp, and they became his voice. She understood he was gone, but she needed to hold onto the memories they had made together.

Sharon never fully recovered from the loss of her child either. Every night in her prayers she whispered, "I love you" to the child she never had the chance to raise. She would take the pink receiving blanket from the drawer and clutch it tightly to her breast and pray that Jesus would take care of His littlest angel until she could once again hold her baby in her arms. Sharon believed that someday when she entered the gate of heaven, she would hold Johnnie Marie in her arms again. This belief was the one thing that kept her going.

They say time heals all wounds, and Sharon moved forward with her life praying this was so. Admittedly, to some degree, it was. She had a life now and she was working with children, and that was her passion. When she went home at night, Future would meet her at the door always giving her unconditional love. He was her companion and friend. When Bobby gave the puppy to her, she learned how to love again. Bobby and Future saved her life. They were her lifeline, and Jesus had saved her soul.

During her second year of teaching, she met Ben. He was a kind, giving man who loved children and worked teaching and coaching them. He was drawn to Sharon from the first time he saw her, and he knew she was the woman he'd been looking for.

This caught Sharon off guard. She wasn't looking for a man in her life and made it clear right from the beginning that she had a lot of baggage to deal with, and it might be in his best interests not to make that leap. But Ben was absolutely sure Sharon was the right woman for him, and he set out to prove this fact to her. One by one, Ben tore down all of the walls Sharon had built around herself over the years, and finally he managed to convince her that he was right. A year after they met, Sharon and Ben were married, and they took Future and bought a home. Two years later, Sharon gave birth to their son, David.

When Sharon first held her son, she felt as if her prayers had been answered. No, he wasn't a replacement for Johnnie Marie, but she felt all of those things every mother feels the first time she holds her baby in her arms. This brought her a great deal of comfort, joy, and peace. David was the focus of her life now, and she knew he was also truly a gift from God. She and Ben were very happy.

Ben knew everything about John and Johnnie Marie, and he was always considerate of Sharon's feelings about that part of her life. He understood the place they held in her heart, but he also knew he had his own place in her heart that only he could fill. When Sharon and Ben began their life together,

Sharon put John's picture in a box, along with the engagement ring John had given her, the heart charm necklace, and all of the letters he sent to her from boot camp, and then placed them on a shelf in the closet. Although they were things Sharon wanted to keep, they became a part of the past. Now Ben was her future, and Sharon and Ben were good together. They were happy together. Somehow, they just seemed to fit.

Still, as Sharon had every night over the past years, she prayed for her daughter and asked Jesus to take care of his littlest angel. She kept the pink blanket in the drawer of her dresser, and Sharon would still pick it up and hold it close to her heart. Ben knew Johnnie Marie was a loss that would always be with Sharon, and he understood that, often offering her comfort when she needed it. Johnnie Marie's birthdays were particularly difficult for her, as she would think about what she might be doing if she were still here. Even though Sharon didn't intend to dwell on those things, sometimes she couldn't help herself. She often prayed these feelings would fade, but they didn't.

Ben and David were now Sharon's life, and she loved both of them deeply. She thanked God for every moment she had with them, and always said, "I love you" and "you're important to me." Sharon prayed she'd never again have to experience the kind of loss she experienced earlier in her life.

As the years passed, David became the joy in Sharon's father's life. Her father was frail now. He had many health problems and had to retire far sooner than he had planned. David filled those years with love for him and brought out a degree of tenderness in her father Sharon had never seen before. David was very close to his grandfather and this was comforting to Sharon.

As time went on, when someone would mention Johnnie Marie around Sharon's father, they noticed sadness would sweep across his face, and this old man who had never before shown emotion about much of anything, would get tears in his eyes. Sharon thought perhaps he had mellowed with age, and thanked Jesus for the tenderness he was now able to show. In a way it was almost comforting to Sharon to think that her father might be thinking about Johnnie Marie and what she might be like now if she had lived.

With a failing heart and a body riddled with disease, her father knew the end was drawing near, and he called his family to his bedside one night needing to settle some things in his mind. He wanted to put to rest some of the mistakes he felt he needed to atone for in his life and wanted his family to know that he loved them, even though he never quite figured out how to show it or say it. He knew he could have been a better father and dearly wished he had been. He wanted Sharon and Ben to know that David was the light of his life, and he told Bobby and his wife Angela that he loved them. He actually said the words.

As Sharon's father lay in the bed very close to the end of his life, he asked forgiveness for all of the mistakes he'd made over the years, and of course his family was ready and willing to forgive everything he may have done. All of them assured him that all was forgiven and he shouldn't give any more thought to it.

Still, he was so agitated and fretful as he lay waiting for the end. Sharon wiped his forehead with a cool cloth and whispered that she loved him in an effort to ease his mind. Crying, he told them he had done something secretly that had haunted him from the day he did it, and now he had to tell them what he had done. Thinking he was no longer aware of what he was saying, his family tried to comfort him again, telling him they loved him and all was forgiven.

It was at that point that he made a confession that shocked and horrified his entire family. None of them were prepared to hear this, least of all Sharon. Out of the need to clear his conscience, Sharon's father reached from deep within himself, looked into his daughter's eyes, and told her what he had done.

As her father reached out to Sharon with a feeble hand, he confessed, "Sharon, I have done an unforgivable thing to you. I can't change it. I can't make it right. It's far too late for that. I pray God will forgive me, although I can't forgive myself. I hope that someday you can find it in your heart to forgive me, Sharon." With tears in his eyes, and in a very weak voice, he continued to speak, forcing himself to say what he had hidden from all of them for so many years. He said, "When I took Johnnie Marie and told you I buried her to save you the pain and grief of having to do it, I lied to you. I lied to your mother. Oh dear God in heaven, how could I have done this thing to you, to all of us?"

As tears rolled down his face, he choked on the words he had, until now, left unspoken. With his last bit of strength he fought to make his confession, now more that thirty years after the fact. The deed he had hidden from all of them he was now struggling to reveal before it was too late. Her father admitted, "I took Johnnie Marie from the hospital and gave her to a man who had a daughter who was desperate to have a child. I paid the doctor to lie and a nurse to cover up the truth. Johnnie Marie isn't dead, Sharon. She was given to someone who wanted her as much as you did. I told myself I did it for you, because you were so very young. I convinced myself it was best for everybody. The truth is, I was ashamed of her, of you, of all of it. Oh my God, how could I have done this? Forgive me. Sharon, say you'll forgive me."

This confession took all of them by total surprise. Struck silent by shock, all of them stood by this man's bedside unable to say or do anything. Sharon trembled and Ben helped her to a chair before she could fall to the floor. Obviously Sharon was totally unprepared to hear this. After thirty years of grieving for her child, she finds out Johnnie Marie was alive, and her father knew it all the time. He watched her go through all of that hell and misery for all those years, and until now, said nothing. How could he have done this? What kind of monster would do this to his child?

13

Ben, realizing Sharon would need to know things she couldn't ask for herself at the moment, leaned over the dying man and questioned, "Where is Johnnie Marie? Who did you give her to? Help us find her. You need to do this for Sharon. Where is she?"

"She was raised seventy miles from the hospital where she was born. I gave her to Peter Holmann so he could give the baby to his daughter and her husband, Laurie and Ray Richards. They thought it was a private legal adoption. They never knew the truth. No one knew, except Peter and me."

Sharon's father took another deep, gasping breath, and made his final request. He asked that Sharon would forgive him. Still shocked, speechless, aching in her heart for the lost years with her daughter, she sat at her father's side trying to say I forgive you, knowing she wasn't sure she honestly could, now or ever.

Pulling together every ounce of strength she had, Sharon reached out to touch her father's hand, and choking on the words as they came from her throat, she said, "I forgive you," as her father took that last final breath. As she sat there, still in shock, numb from the revelation which had unfolded before her only moments before, Sharon tearfully whispered, "Jesus, forgive me for the lie I just told my father. I pray someday I will truly be able to forgive him for this unforgivable act. I just know it's not today. God forgive me." Sobbing uncontrollably, Sharon looked at each of her family members and realized all of them were as shocked and horrified as she was over her father's confession.

Sharon's mother had never known about this. Her husband never spoke a word about it to her. When he had Johnnie Marie buried, he had the little casket sealed and told her it was too difficult to see, and she would be much better off remembering the baby alive and in her mother's arms, rather than in that casket. He seemed so sincere that she never questioned his judgment on the matter. She never knew he lied. How could he have done this? Sharon's mother was as crushed by the truth as was Sharon. How could he have done this? How?

Bobby and Angela felt all of these same things. What kind of man could have done this to his own daughter? He watched her anguish in the pain for years over the death of Johnnie Marie and never said a word. Bobby's heart went out to his sister who would once again have all of the old wounds opened. He prayed this time that she would be able to finally put all of this to rest. He wondered if she would ever be able to forgive their father for having done this terrible thing to her?

Ben held Sharon, consoling her as best he could. Both of them always believed that each will be forgiven by Jesus, the way we forgive others. So where did this leave Sharon? Ben wondered how she would find her way through her father's lies to a place where she would be able to forgive him. He wasn't sure he could forgive this.

Sharon pulled herself together for her mother's sake and helped make her father's funeral arrangements. She would go from being elated that she might be able to see her daughter and be part of her life, to despair over what her father had done, and in pain over all of those lost years with Johnnie Marie. Between the funeral, trying to hold her mother together, and dealing with her father's deathbed confession, Sharon felt as if she were living on an emotional roller coaster.

Ben immediately began a search to find Johnnie Marie using the information Sharon's father had given him. It didn't take long to find answers. He was amazed at how easy it was. The whole time he searched, he just kept thinking about all the years of pain Sharon could have been spared if only her father hadn't done this. How different Sharon's life would have been if he would have told the truth many years ago. As Ben searched, he prayed Johnnie Marie was alive and that Sharon would be able to see her daughter.

The search quickly led to answers. The doctor who delivered Johnnie Marie had died many years ago, as had the nurse. The man who was given the baby was also gone now. Ben tracked down that man's family and then went to them to tell them the whole story. Sharon's father had spoken the truth on his deathbed. Neither Laurie or Ray Richards knew the true circumstances of the adoption.

They had been told the child's mother was unwed, and unable to care for the baby, and wanted to give her the best home possible. They believed her mother had given her up for adoption willingly to insure the child would have a better life. They believed she did this out of love for the baby, not because she didn't want her. This was what they were told, and they both believed it. There was no reason to question it.

Laurie and Ray explained that they had tried for many years to have children but couldn't. Laurie was diagnosed with uterine cancer when she was thirty-five, and they knew they would never be able to have a child of their own. They tried to adopt, but because Laurie had been diagnosed with cancer, and because they were now into their late thirties, adoption was proving to be difficult. Laurie's father arranged for a private adoption. Everything was legal and above board as far as the Richard's knew. When the baby was born, now thirty years ago, Laurie's father came to their home with his lawyer one night and brought this beautiful baby girl to them. They signed some papers. And that was that. They named the baby, Destiny Rose.

Laurie and Ray told Destiny she was adopted. They never made any secret of it. They told her that her mother was a young, unwed teen who didn't have the resources to care for her. They told her it was because her mother loved her so deeply that she gave her baby to someone who would be able to give her everything she couldn't. Destiny had been told that if she ever wanted to find her biological parents, they would help her to do so. She never asked them to, so they never tried.

After Ben told Laurie and Ray the truth about everything, of course, they were shocked and felt very unsure about what to do next. They told Ben they needed a little time to process all of this and asked if they could call him in a few days. Ben agreed. This only seemed fair. After all, they too, had been lied to and deceived by someone they loved and trusted.

Laurie and Ray decided to go to Destiny and tell her all of this. They felt that she should be the one to decide if she wanted to see her biological mother. They believed she would and should see her birth mother but felt this had to be Destiny's decision.

After hearing the whole story, Destiny agreed to meet with her birth mother. She confessed to her parents that she had often wondered about who her biological parents were, but she never wanted to hurt them by starting to look or by asking questions.

Laurie and Ray sat with their daughter and explained they believed she had every right to meet her birth parents if she wanted to. Nothing would ever change the bond of love they shared as a family. They would always be Mom and Dad, and nothing was ever going to change that. Laurie and Ray told her that God loves all of us, and surely each of us can manage to love more than one mother and father.

With the assurance that she would always love Laurie and Ray and that they would always be her real parents, she agreed to meet with Ben and Sharon. The arrangements were made, and Ben brought Sharon to be reunited with her daughter.

Destiny was almost thirty-one now. She had been married for almost nine years to Sam, and they were very happy. They had a son named Craig who was seven, and they were expecting a second child in about two months.

When Laurie and Ray met Sharon and Ben at the airport, the Richards were amazed at how much Destiny looked like her mother. If they had harbored any doubts about the validity of Sharon's story, seeing her dispelled all of them. The resemblance was remarkable.

With all four of them expecting awkward moments at this first meeting, they were pleasantly surprised when everyone seemed so comfortable with the others. Maybe it was their common desire to do what each of them knew was right and best for Destiny. Or maybe it was an answer to their many prays, but whatever it was, it seemed to fit. Sharon and Ben thanked God for that.

When they arrived at Destiny's home, Sharon was nervous. She had feared that her daughter might think she gave her away because she didn't want the responsibility of raising her. Laurie took Sharon's hand and told her that Destiny knew the truth. She had always believed her mother let her go out of love for her. Laurie assured Sharon that their daughter was an amazing, compassionate and loving person, and she had nothing to fear.

Together the four of them walked up to the door. Sharon had never even dared to hope to see Johnnie Marie here on earth and had resigned herself to being reunited with her daughter in heaven. Now only a door separated her from the daughter she believed had died over thirty years ago. Sharon knew Jesus had answered her many prayers. After ringing the doorbell she stood waiting for Destiny.

As Destiny opened the door, there before Sharon stood the daughter she believed she would never again see on earth. Destiny looked at her mother, and as their eyes met, each of them recognized the other. If not for the sixteen years difference in their ages, they were almost the mirror image of one another. Without a word Destiny reached out to Sharon and finally after thirty years of pain, grief, and loss, Sharon once again held her daughter in her arms.

This was so much more than Sharon had even dared to hope for, and she could only whisper, "Thank you, Jesus," through tears of joy and sweet release. The pain of the past thirty years was gone and had been replaced with feelings of love, peace, joy, and comfort. Reaching her hand back toward the others standing behind her, Sharon took Laurie's hand and pulled her into the embrace with Destiny. Soon Ray and Ben enclosed their arms around all three of the women to complete the picture that was way too many years overdue.

Sharon was thankful that Laurie and Ray were the people who had reared her daughter. They had done such a wonderful job because Destiny was truly an incredible person. With so many things to learn about her daughter, she didn't know where to begin. As they sat and talked, they all got answers to questions they had, and they knew that now they would have many more years to get to know one another. Out of love for their daughter, Laurie and Ray were willing to share Destiny with Sharon and Ben.

Destiny was a very talented artist. She drew portraits of people that were beyond beautiful. Sharon told her she must have gotten that talent from John. Destiny had gone to college and graduated at the top of her class. When she was a child, she danced, raced dirt bikes, and had a puppy. Every one of these facts were comforting for Sharon to hear. She saw pictures from Destiny's prom and her wedding.

They talked about Destiny's family and looked at pictures of them. Destiny explained that Sam took their son Craig on a weekend camping trip with a father and son group they belong to. Sam offered to cancel and stay home with her, but she thought this might be the best way to do this anyway. Now she was wishing she had asked them to stay home. But Sharon and Ben assured Destiny that they would all have years together to get to know one another, and reminded her that she would also have to get to know her brother, David. There would be time for all of this.

They continued to talk about Destiny's childhood, and she told Sharon that when she was eight she fell out of a boat and into the lake at summer camp and almost drowned. If not for the efforts of a mysterious young man who dove in the water and pulled her to safety, she would have died. She never found out who he was, but later she came to believe that he was her guardian angel.

Destiny went on to explain that when she was seventeen, while driving home one night, a drunken driver hit her car forcing it off the road and down an embankment. The car rolled over and then caught on fire. She was trapped inside and couldn't get out of the car no matter how hard she tried, and again this same young stranger came to her rescue. He pulled her out of the car, saving her life for a second time. People saw him do this, but no one knew who he was or where he went afterward, and she hasn't seen him since that night.

She said, when she left the hospital following that accident, along with her watch and clothes, there was a gold necklace with a charm shaped like a heart torn in half. She told the people at the hospital they made a mistake and that the necklace didn't belong to her. But the doctor who was on call in the emergency room when she was brought in, said he removed the necklace from around her neck when he went to treat her wounds. He remembered it very clearly, so Destiny kept it.

Destiny also said she had drawn a picture of the man who saved her back when she was eight and then decided to paint a portrait of him after the second incident. When she offered to show Sharon and Ben both the sketched picture and the portrait of her hero, of course they wanted to see them. Following Destiny into the den in her home, Sharon and Ben were completely dumbfounded when they saw the painting titled *Destiny's Guardian Angel*. Aside from the fact that the painting was beautiful, it was also remarkable in another way. Around the neck of the subject of this painting, Destiny had drawn the gold half heart necklace she described.

Ben asked Ray to help him get something out of the car and both men went out to find it. Ben knew Sharon wanted to show this to her daughter, and he knew this was the right time to do it. When they returned, Ben was carrying a box. He set it on the coffee table in the den and Sharon opened it. From within the box, Sharon removed something wrapped in tissue paper, and after she removed the paper, she walked over and handed the framed picture to Destiny.

With tears rolling down her face, Sharon said, "Johnnie Marie, sweetheart, this is your father, John."

Destiny took the picture from her mother's hands and looked down at it. Breathlessly she whispered, "Oh, Mom, Dad, look at this. My guardian angel, he's my father. Oh, I can't believe this. I don't know what to say. He's my father."

Sharon went on to explain that she never had the chance to tell John that he was going to be a father before he was killed, so the truth is, he didn't know about Johnnie Marie at all. Now, thirty years later, Sharon knew that John had been watching over their daughter for all of those years. Jesus had answered her prayers from the beginning.

Ben looked into the box and removed a smaller box from it and handed it to Sharon. She kissed his cheek gently and thanked him as he handed the box to her. Then she gave the box to Destiny.

Destiny opened it and then removed a gold chain with a half heart charm. She reached inside her sweater and pulled out a chain she had around her own neck and revealed the other half of the heart. Placing the two halves of the heart together, Destiny read the inscription, "*One Heart Forever Joined With Love.*" She then continued to explain, "I believed my guardian angel had given it to me after he pulled me from the burning car, and I've worn it ever since the day I left the hospital. That was thirteen years ago now. It was a gift from my father and until now, I never knew it. My guardian angel did give this to me. I always believed he had, but now I know it's true. The handsome young stranger was my father. Oh Mom. Daddy look at this," Destiny said while showing her parents the heart. "Oh, thank you Jesus for this gift. Thank you for uniting my family," Destiny cried as tears of joy rolled down her face.

That day all of these people became bonded for life. There were so many things each of them wanted to know about the other, and now they would have years to learn everything. This was a new beginning for all of them.

Destiny now had two mothers (Laurie and Sharon), and three fathers (Ray, Ben, and John; who is also her guardian angel, as well as her biological father). She has a brother named David to whom she has become very close.

Two months later Destiny and Sam had a beautiful baby girl. Craig was so impressed with his brand new little sister he couldn't wait to show her off to all of his grandparents, including Sharon and Ben.

When Sharon and Ben arrived at the hospital for the first time to see their second grandchild, Destiny and Sam had a surprise waiting for them. Craig and David had helped to plan the surprise, and Laurie and Ray were gathered there with the others waiting, too. With the video recorder on, Destiny handed the baby to Sharon and Ben and said, "Mom and Dad, we want you to meet your first granddaughter; her name is Johnnie Marie. I know she's going to love you as much as we do. We thank God that you're part of our lives."

As Sharon held her granddaughter in her arms she cried tears of joy and thanked God for the many blessings in her life. Standing there, surrounded by the people she loved most in this world, knowing her prayers had been answered, Sharon raised her eyes up toward heaven and whispered, " Daddy, I forgive you."

With that Sharon closed the door on a painful chapter in her life. What she once thought was unforgivable, had now been forgiven. Recognizing she did not have the right to stand in judgement of her father and the deed he committed more than thirty years ago, she was able to forgive him completely. She knew Jesus would want it this way.

♥ ♥ ♥ ♥ ♥ ♥ ♥

Linda C. Luebke

I pray that all of us will think very carefully and ask Jesus for guidance before we do anything that might impact the lives of others so significantly as Sharon's father's decision and actions impacted her life. I'm amazed at what some of us do, supposedly, in the name of love...

After meeting Sharon at one of the signings for my first book, she called me and told me about her story. It was her belief that her story could help someone else by showing them that Jesus hears all of our prayers, and He does answer them. It may not be an immediate or instant response, but He does answers our prayers in His own time, and in His own way.

If we'll have faith and believe the promises Jesus made to all of us, He'll never let us down. We need to take our burdens to the Lord, leave them with Him, and have faith He will help us. We must learn to be patient and wait.

We also, in Jesus name, must ask to be forgiven for our sins, and then forgive those who transgress against us. We are forgiven in the same way we chose to forgive others. None of us can escape this truth.

Not all of the problems and trials we will face in this world will have happy endings. Each of us has been given free a will, and unfortunately, not everyone will choose to follow Jesus. There will be those who will choose to follow Satan, others who will decide to follow no one, and still some that do not believe that God exists at all. Everyone must make this choice for themselves. Unfortunately, when people make those kinds of choices, they can and do impact the lives of others. Remembering it's God's will that must be done, we need to wait to see which way He may choose to answer our prayers. The one constant here is that He will answer us.

One really good thing about knowing and accepting Jesus as your personal Savior is that there is nothing you can do that He won't forgive. If when you ask forgiveness and you are honestly sorry for what you've done, He'll always forgive you, wash you clean, and then forget about what you did wrong. Once you're forgiven by Jesus He doesn't remember your sin. He doesn't hold a grudge, and He doesn't seek revenge. Jesus' forgiveness is total, complete and forever. It's important to remember that we must be truly remorseful, repent and than go on and do better. Jesus knows what is in your heart. He sees all.

I've heard people say, "I'll forgive you, but I won't forget it." Is this the way your want to be forgiven? I know I wouldn't want Jesus to remember all of my mistakes, sins and bad choices. We need to learn by the example Jesus set for us, and follow what He says in the Bible. Without forgiving others the way Jesus forgives us, we will never find inner peace.

I know I've done things in my life I wish I hadn't done. In those cases I when I stepped forward and did what I could do to make things right, I felt better within myself. I believe I've learned from those mistakes and try not to repeat them. It is my belief that Jesus wants all of us to love and care for one another in the same way He loves and cares for each of us. I truly do thank Him for that gift of His great love.

20

Lord Rest My Soul

I need a place to rest my soul. Lord I'm tired and I'm weak.
Today I've lost something I need, and now it's your love that I seek.
Lord, touch me with compassion, hold my soul and light my way.
Without you I would go under, so in Jesus name I pray...

Hold me through this night, keep me safe from harm.
Light the pathway that you want me to take.
Grant me peace of mind as you lead me through this life.
I will follow, Lord, if you will lead my way.
Stepping out on faith, in Jesus name I pray...

With faith I'm reaching out to you knowing you will hear my call.
Your Spirit lifts my soul. Your love will help me through it all.
There's nothing I can't conquer, Jesus, if you will be my shield.
Sowing seeds of love for the Master, I pray, is what my life will yield.

Hold me through this night, keep me safe from harm.
Light the pathway that you want me to take.
Grant me peace of mind as you lead me through this life.
I will follow, Lord, if you will lead my way.
Stepping out on faith, in Jesus name I pray...

Lord, you're the place to rest my soul. With forgiveness you wash me clean.
With faith renewed, and peace of mind, I've found just what I need.
Because He chose to do these things, we have a trilogy of hope.
For hope is Our Father in Heaven, Jesus Christ the Son, and the Holy Ghost.

The course of our lives is not mapped out for us in heaven. All of us have free a will and we must find our way through this world. Some of us will have more problems along the way than others of us might have. But God will help each of us, if we will ask Him for His help and believe He will give it to us.

I posted the next poem on the my website one day and a few days later, I received an e-mail from a man who told me this poem told his life story. He explained how he'd lost everything because of his relationship with the bottle. Before he was able to find his way through the haze of blurred memory and drunken rage, he destroyed everything around him. He lost his wife, his children, his home and his job.

Finally one day he found Jesus and slowly he began to turn his life around. The alcohol very nearly killed him before he could fight his way through the destruction, and into Jesus loving embrace. Now he has devoted his life to helping others with similar problems. He prays that someday his family will recognize that he, too, has become a better man.

A Better Man

He woke up in the morning to a silence he'd never heard before.
No giggling, laughing children. No Mom saying,
"Hush now, Daddy will hear." Unsure of "why" the silence,
With an aching head he stumbles out of bed.
There in the kitchen lay the explanation,
And the one thing he'd most feared.

Reflecting on the night before, he remembers a drunken, angry rage.
A flash of fear and pain drift across his memory;
It's the look on his wife's face.
Like broken glass the pieces of their
Shattered lives lay scattered on the floor.
And on the table is a note saying simply, "I can't take this any more."

With tears streaming down his face,
He reaches out for the telephone. But there is only silence,
He remembers; he'd pulled the cord out of the wall.
Where could she have gone? How could she take his children away?
Then emptiness strikes fear into his heart for he knows;
How could she have stayed?

Dropping to his knees in desperation,
He cries out to our Father in pain. "Lord, forgive the fool I am.
Jesus, please help me to be a better man.
How could I have lost sight of everything I once believed I should be?
How could I drive away the love and trust
My family once held for me?"

Now two years later he still struggles
With the ghost from the bottle in his past.
Where Jesus has forgiven him,
Somehow he finds it hard to forgive himself.
Armed with the Bible and a prayer,
He prays that someday they will understand.
With the bottle in his past, his faith in God renewed,
He has become a better man...

22

I've always felt and known the love of God. He was present in the earliest thoughts and memories I had as a child. As far back as I can remember, Jesus has played an important role in my life. I understand this may seem odd to some of you, but it is true. I've never questioned or doubted that God lives, or that Jesus is with me. I am truly a believer and have no memory of a time in my life when this was not true.

I've often wondered what it was that drew me to Him so completely, and in such a way as to never question God's never ending love and grace. I'm relatively certain I won't know the answer to this question until I go to heaven, but then again, one never knows? I can say this, knowing the Lord had given me peace beyond comprehension.

Have You Heard?

I know something I think that you should know.
There is someone who truly loves you.
I know it's true, for He really loves me, too.
He has touched my soul and now,
He will touch yours, too.

With love He sweeps across our lives and clears our doubts away.
He lights our pathway through the night. Our burdens He will take.
With compassion He forgives our past and makes us clean again.
He grants us love, faith, and peace of mind,
He saves the souls of man throughout all time.

I have seen something I thought I would never see.
It is the power of the love my Jesus has for me.
Now I feel something I thought I'd never feel.
Compassion from within my soul
Bids me to do His will.

With love He sweeps across our lives and wipes our doubts away.
He lights our pathway through the night. Our burdens, He, will take.
With compassion He forgives our past and makes us clean again.
He grants us love, faith, and peace of mind,
He saves the souls of man throughout all time.

I have done something I thought I'd never do.
My soul has touched the face of God. My spirit is renewed...

Linda C. Luebke

The Garden

As Jenny pulled into the driveway, she noticed that everything looked the same somehow. This was the same home she'd lived in for the past thirty-four years and to all outward appearances, nothing had changed. But looks can be deceiving and she knew nothing would ever be the same again. As she turned the car engine off, she thought about all the times she had done this exact same thing before. This seemed so familiar and still she knew now, today, this time; it was very different. Taking a deep breath, she summoned every ounce of courage she could find, pushed the car door open and stepped out.

When she got to the front door, Jenny stood almost paralyzed, as if she were trying to force the inevitable away from her. As her key found its way into the lock, she felt a tear start to roll down her face. She wondered how her life could have taken such a drastic turn. As she pushed the door open she saw her home stretched out before her; as empty as she felt.

The tears were now streaming down her face and that awful lump in her throat had grown so large, she felt as if she would choke on it. Her throat ached. Her heart ached. Closing the door behind her, she entered the house knowing she must confront the ghosts that dwell within her mind, her heart, and those walls.

As the sun danced through the window of the living room, Jenny walked over to the window seat and sat down. She kicked her shoes off and pulled her feet up and turned her body so she could look out the window and into the back yard garden. She and her husband had made that garden together. This had always been her favorite spot in the house, and she felt some comfort as she sat looking out of the window.

Jenny believed she had the typical, average American life. Her husband Greg was a loving, caring, generous man who adored her and their children. They had two, Amanda, age twenty-eight; and Bret who would have been twenty now, if life could have gone on the way Jenny thought life should be. But, it didn't.

Today Jenny sat quietly on the window seat and wondered if there was anything she could have done to have changed or altered the chain of events that brought her and her family to this place in time. She had so many questions, and way too few answers. If not for her faith in God, Jenny would have lost her mind, and her soul, long ago. Her faith is the only reason she is here today.

Jenny and Greg married after he finished college and took a position in his family's business. She had completed her second year of college and decided to put her education on hold for a couple of years to marry Greg and hopefully start a family. The beginning years of their marriage were rather typical and their relationship was quite strong and pretty normal. Yes, they had some rough spots and hit a few bumps in the road, but all things considered, they were happily married.

When they married, they bought a house they felt they could afford. It was an older home and Jenny and Greg thought it had a lot of character and possibility. This became a labor of love. They worked tirelessly on it for three years to turn it into their dream home. Having conquered the inside of their home successfully, they turned their attention to the lawn and back yard garden that had been left unattended for many years prior to their purchase of the house.

Both Greg and Jenny knew the back yard garden would be a lifetime commitment, but they both felt it would be worth all of the effort they would have to put into it over the years. They worked very hard to make it beautiful once again. They did succeed in their task, and the garden was finally lovely, although they both understood it would require a lot of tending to keep it that way.

The timing in their lives seemed to be right on target. As their home was finally finished inside and out, Jenny learned she was pregnant. Greg and Jenny decorated the nursery in the anticipation of their newest project. When Amanda was born, she was their pride and joy. She was a beautiful little girl and by all accounts, had a loving and gentle disposition. Amanda was very bright and sweet. She started school already knowing most everything she was sent there to learn. She breezed through it effortlessly. Jenny and Greg were very proud of her.

When Amanda was seven, Jenny became pregnant with her second child. Amanda was thrilled. She had often said she wanted a little brother or sister. All of her friends had one, and she was finally going to have one, too. This was a joyous event in all of their lives. The entire family was looking forward to the arrival of their little package from heaven.

Where Jenny's first pregnancy was easy and went well, this one was more difficult and some of the problems became frightening for both Jenny and Greg. She had morning sickness all the time, and had some bleeding three times during the first seven months. Jenny went into labor twice, way too early, but with the help of the doctors, some medications and a whole lot of prayers, she managed to carry the baby eight months. She spent most of the pregnancy in bed.

It was at this time in Jenny's life that she turned to God. She had always been a Christian, at least on the surface. But during this time, she really reached out to Jesus, and He answered. Both she and Greg found a new beginning in their lives. Where it's true they both reached out to Jesus out of desperation and fear for their unborn child, they both made a permanent connection to Jesus.

By the time Bret was born, he was welcomed into a loving, Christian family. His sister, Amanda, adored her baby brother and couldn't get enough of him. Greg had his son, the light of his life. And Jenny had her little boy. He was perfect. Everything about him was special to all of them. Bret and Amanda were always close. This was true from the day Bret was born and remained so throughout his life.

Bret was small from the beginning. Where he weighed all of barely four pounds at birth, he was very strong and extremely active. He always seemed to be on the move. When he was tiny his little feet and hands moved constantly, and later when he learned to walk, he ran. The busier he could be, the better he liked it. He was always helping to do something for someone. Bret was mom's best little helper everyday. Amanda never had to ask her brother to help her. If he saw a need, it was done. He couldn't do enough for his dad either. Whether it was working around the house, or out in the yard, Bret was the first one to start and the last one to stop. You could always depend on him to be there side by side with his dad. As Bret grew older, these things didn't change, at least in the beginning.

The family often worked and played in the garden. Everyone did his or her part to keep it beautiful. Often Bret played out there and Amanda would go out to watch him. Bret had a very active imagination and as children will, pretended to be king, or a hero or dragon slayer; and in his mind cast his older sister in the role of damsels in distress. Being older, Amanda would often go along with his game of the day, just to keep him happy. They were two normal, happy children doing all the things you might find most normal happy children doing.

Jenny and Greg thought life was wonderful. Greg was moving up in the family business and they were financially stable and all seemed right in their world. Jenny was preparing to go back to college because Bret had mastered both preschool and kindergarten, and was starting first grade. Amanda was in junior high school.

As the children grew older, Amanda's interests and life began to change. She was busy being a teenager, and doing all of the things girls her age were doing. But, she always made time for Bret in her life, although not in the same way she once did. She knew Bret missed having things the way they once were, but he seemed to be going on with his own life; as one would expect he would. He made new friends and got along well with others. Bret often had friends come over to play. He was always willing to help anyone who needed help. That was just the kind of person he was, helpful, loving and kind.

When Bret started first grade, his lessons didn't come as easy to him as they had in preschool and kindergarten. He struggled to learn things that seemed much easier for his classmates to grasp. This was such a drastic change from the last two years he was in school. No one could understand what was going on with him. Most of what they were doing was simply review of what he already knew. Still he struggled. As his grades worsened, so did his behavior and attitude. The teachers called, complaining Bret's behavior was disruptive in class and he was hurting other children. This wasn't at all like him. It was as if he had suddenly become someone else, a stranger. His grades were bad and his teachers thought counseling might help.

Jenny noticed other changes in Bret's behavior at home too. He was becoming more introverted; less friendly with other children and seemed to be pulling away from his family. He would often go into his room and sit alone for hours. This was so unlike him. He stopped having his little friends come over to the house to play and if they would call to invite him to their homes, he'd say he was tired, or busy, or just didn't want to go. Jenny and Greg felt as if they were living in someone else's nightmare. Jenny stopped going to college and devoted all of her time to helping her son, who was losing ground daily. Jenny and Greg tried everything they could to help their son, but nothing seemed to help. Bret was moody, angry, cold, indifferent and, sometimes, even violent.

All of these things took place gradually over a period of three years. His grades were poor, but passing. He lost interest in helping his father around the house, refusing to do much of anything at all. He would have sudden and unexplained outbursts of anger toward his sister and his mother. Often he would hit one of them for no apparent reason. He'd always apologize for his actions, when told to do so and then go into his room alone. When Jenny or Greg would go to his room to check on him, they would often find him sitting on the floor just rocking back and forth. On occasion, they heard Bret talking to himself, kind of mumbling under his breath. None of this made any sense. Clearly this was a child in trouble, but why? What was going on?

In the beginning, Amanda tried to make excuses for her brother's behavior and mood swings. She always tried to be the one person he could come to when he needed a friend. She always tried to help Bret, but in time even she had to accept the fact that his behavior wasn't going to improve, at least not any time soon. Still, she stayed close to her brother, or at least as close as anyone could dare to get.

Jenny and Greg had Bret go to counseling in school, but this didn't seem to help. They took him to the pediatrician several times looking for answers. Physically Bret seemed fine. Emotionally and mentally something was wrong. They enlisted the help of a child psychologist, who in the beginning also had no answers. Finally, after five years of therapy and testing, the psychologist told Jenny and Greg he believed Bret was suffering from severe depression. He referred to it as bipolar disorder, or possibly schizophrenia, which would be extremely rare in someone so young. The doctor explained this is very rare in children, but he thought Bret might be helped with new medications. They began treating him with some of these. Finding the right one, or combination of medications, can be very difficult and can take a long time. They prayed about this and knew Jesus would help Bret.

Bret, now nearing the end of the fifth grade, on this new medication, was finally reverting back to the Bret everyone once knew and loved. He was once again becoming friendly, outgoing, gentle and caring. His grades bounced back and he was getting A's and B's. He started to make friends with other children again and was becoming more playful and loving with his sister, Amanda.

Jenny had spent the past five and a half years of her life trying to help her son, and finally her prayers were answered. She believed Jesus had finally led the doctor to the right medicine. Bret was better. It took several more months to see the results, but finally they did see them. He was well for the first time in almost six years. Amanda had her loving little brother back. Greg had his son, his little helper. Jenny felt at peace. This was the first time in almost six years she could really see progress. Her faith in God had brought her through all of this. Her son was going to be fine now. She was sure of it. She praised Jesus outwardly, as did her husband. Jenny finally recognized her son of long ago. It was as if the old Bret was back and the Bret with all of the problems had vanished.

During the time Bret was so ill, no one in the family really tended the garden. It was somewhat kept up in bits and pieces, but largely, it had become overgrown with weeds and not really cared for properly. So too, were the relationships of the entire family. Amanda was now a beautiful young woman who would soon graduate from high school and go away to college. No longer the little girl she was when her brother became ill, she felt as if she had missed many things in her own life because of Bret's illness and the entire situation she and her family faced. But, she never stopped loving Bret or gave up on him. She was always very supportive and loving toward him. She loved her brother and vowed never to lose him in that way again. She and Bret once again became very close. Bret seemed relieved to finally able to feel something special for her again. He stopped isolating himself from the rest of the world and appeared to have some balance in his life.

Greg had all but lost his son for several years and wanted to rebuild the relationship with him. Slowly, they began picking up the pieces of their lives, and, hand in hand, they started to find their way back to one another. The old house was in a state of disrepair. But together, father and son made the necessary repairs, both on the house and on themselves. Each of them, taking care of the other's needs first. Gently and slowly they repaired the bond of love and trust between them.

Jenny had never given up on her son, and Bret knew this. He loved his mother deeply. He owed his life to her. This was a bond that was never broken. Jenny would often tell Bret stories about Jesus and the miracles He performed when He walked on this earth. In her soul she always believed Jesus would do one for Bret too.

Jenny and Greg's marriage was also left unattended through those years. They had drifted apart to some degree, but both felt the relationship was worth any work it might take to pull it back together. Slowly they began the process of getting to know one another again. Both of them began reaffirming their faith in God and their faith in one another. With time, the pieces fell back into place.

Soon they were all back together as a real family. Amanda decided to attend college close to home, so she would be able to remain close to her family. She wanted Bret to know she would always be there for him and being physically close to home would seem to be one way she could reassure him. This family had been divided too long.

They all began to tend the garden of life together. In the Bible we read, "What you sow is what you reap." Jenny knew she must keep her faith in God first and foremost in her life, and by her example and faith, her children would learn about the wonders of Jesus too. For the first time in a very long time, life was easier for the entire family. Several years passed and they were blessed many times over for their faith.

Jenny and Greg renewed their wedding vows alone one night as they sat beside their fireplace. Both of them realized how little time they had spent together during the past few years and recognized how truly blessed they were to have found their way through everything that had happened, and managed to have come out of this together. If anything, they believed their bond of love, faith and trust was stronger now than ever before.

Life went well for all of them for about the next seven years. Amanda graduated from college, married her college sweetheart and gave Jenny and Greg the first of their two grandchildren, a beautiful baby girl Amanda and Ross named Beth Ann. Beth was a joy and a treasure for everyone. Bret loved this little girl, heart and soul. He spent as much time as possible with her, as did Jenny and Greg.

Bret graduated from high school and was planning to attend college in the fall. He wanted to be an author and journalist. He had been in all the school plays and had even written a couple. He was very talented and had a way with the written word. This was his passion. Jenny had often thought Bret's writing was good therapy for him.

The medications the doctor had found for him made his life, and everyone else's, easier. If the depression came back at him over those years, know one ever knew it. Bret seemed to be very happy and was looking forward to going to college and life in general.

He had a girlfriend who knew about his past problems and chose to be with him in spite of them. Her name is Deanna. She planned to go to college, also. Where they didn't plan to attend the same school, they expected to continue the relationship. Both of them were very happy and they were looking forward to a bright future. Deanna was Bret's first love and Jenny didn't know if it would stand the test of time, but she knew he was happy.

Bret was a Christian. He believed Jesus saved his life and his soul. He was very open about this and lived a life his Lord and Savior could be proud of. He and Deanna were both believers. If there was anything wrong in Bret's life, there were no outward signs of it. He took his medication every day, saw his doctor on a regular basis, got along well with his family and friends. Bret was close to Deanna and looking forward to getting to know her better. He was devoted to his belief in God. The problems Bret encountered earlier in his life were now a distant memory; or so it would seem.

As Jenny sat on the window seat overlooking the garden, she could remember the last time she saw Bret. Deanna had come over to the house to have dinner with the family. It was Friday night and all of them had just finished eating and were about ready to start cleaning the kitchen. Bret insisted all the "young folks" should do the dishes and had ushered both Jenny and Greg out of the kitchen. But Jenny never could stay out of her kitchen leaving someone else in charge, so she wandered back in just in time to catch Bret and Deanna in an embrace. Greg was just behind Jenny as they opened the door and saw this tender moment between the young couple. Greg joked with Bret about being careful not to get any of those "girl germs" on him because they don't wash off all that easily. Everyone laughed. Amanda and Ross were over by the sink trying to get a stain out of little Beth's dress.

Bret loved Beth Ann. Amanda said she and Ross chose her name, because it was so similar to her brother's name, Bret Andrew. He went over to the sink and scooped Beth up in his arms and gave her a big kiss. Then he and Deanna took the stained dress off their little angel and handed it to Amanda and Ross, telling them, "Beth Ann has more important things to do than be on the old stain removal committee." Bret and Deanna continued to play with Beth for the better part of an hour.

Jenny remembered it was almost 9:00 p.m. when Amanda and Ross said their good-byes and left for home with little Beth Ann. Bret was still living at home, but said, "Good night. I love you." Then he went out the door to take Deanna home. Jenny and Greg settled in to relax in front of the fire. They had just spent quality time with their family and all was right with the world. They sat there together for quite a while watching the flames dance across the logs. Greg commented on how mesmerizing the flames were. At about 10:30 p.m. Jenny and Greg went up to bed.

At 7:00 a.m. the phone rang and Jenny remembered sleepily answering it to hear her daughter on the other end. Amanda told her that Beth had spiked a high temperature over night and she was going to run into the clinic with her.

Beth was prone to ear infections and it was assumed this was just one more of many. In any case Amanda just wanted to let Jenny know what was going on.

Greg climbed out of bed as Jenny went downstairs to the kitchen to make coffee. As she passed Bret's bedroom she noticed his bed hadn't been slept in. Okay, this wasn't the first time this happened and she just assumed he ended up spending the night at Deanna's house. Jenny could remember saying to herself; "this was inevitable."

Jenny and Greg had breakfast and planned to spend the day getting caught up with some of the yard work and gardening. The sun was shining and both of them were outside working when a police officer and another gentleman came walking up the driveway. They approached Greg first. Jenny knew by the look on his face; something was terribly wrong. She got up off her knees and ran toward her husband. The officer told her that Bret was dead.

Jenny went completely numb. If anything else was stated at that point in time, she didn't hear it. She couldn't think or move. She could barely breathe. She can remember thinking and screaming, "No. It can't be Bret. No. I don't believe this! You're wrong, you have to be."

The next few days were a blur. Jenny had difficulty remembering them at all. Something happened to her when her son died. Her heart was broken, and so too was her mind and spirit. It was as if she died too. All she could think or feel was pain. Every thought, every breath, every moment was unbearable. Agony! She couldn't see Greg's pain, or Amanda's, and certainly not Deanna's. Jenny can remember feeling that she wished she were dead. She really wanted to lay down and die.

The details of Bret's death were sketchy, at best. The police said it appeared to be a suicide. Suicide, no way! Why? How? This didn't make any sense! Bret had conquered his demons long ago. The mental illness was under control for over seven years. He took his medication daily and didn't seem depressed at all. He showed no outward symptoms of anything being wrong. Jenny was convinced it could not have been suicide.

Just last night he had been joking around in the kitchen with his family. Bret had been laughing and playing with Beth Ann, holding Deana in his arms and behaving as if he didn't have a care in the world. This just didn't fit. When he left the house to take Deanna home he said, "Good night. I love you." This doesn't sound like someone who is going off to kill himself. Jenny couldn't believe this. It simply wasn't possible.

According to the initial police report the investigators believed Bret had taken his own life. He allegedly used a .22 caliber handgun to inflict a single gunshot wound to the right temple of his head. The approximate time of death was between 11:30 p.m. on Friday night, and 1:30 a.m. on Saturday morning when a patrol car stopped behind a vehicle parked on the side of the road and found a body slumped over the steering wheel. The motor was turned off and the vehicle's transmission was in park. The car doors were locked, but the driver's side window was shattered when the bullet passed through Bret's head from the right temple exiting the left rear side of his head and through the window. Two days following his death, the coroner confirmed Bret died from a single self-inflicted gunshot wound to the head.

Jenny fought desperately to understand how this could have happened. Bret didn't own a gun. Greg never had one in the house. Where did the weapon come from? Why would Bret do this when his life held such promise? He was looking forward to college and a budding romance with Deanna. Where were the signs that something was wrong? He was happy. He had everything to live for and no reason to take his own life.

As Jenny screamed out to God in pain and disbelief, she could only ask, "Why?" and beg Him to wake her from this nightmare; this hell. But she wasn't dreaming and there were no answers. She couldn't get past the pain. The aftermath of Bret's suicide was evident to everyone around her. Jenny crumbled under the weight of the loss of her son. The devastation she felt shook her very soul and Jenny questioned everything she ever believed or put her faith in.

Somewhere in the back of her mind, she can remember Greg trying to comfort her and share their grief. But at the time Jenny was going through all of this, she could only feel the pain of the loss of her only son. She lost sight of the fact that Bret was Greg's only son also. He needed her and he also needed to help her. Jenny pushed everyone away and seemed to fold her life into herself and shut out everything around her. She felt only pain and grief, and nothing else. Looking back on it now, Jenny realizes how incredibly alone and helpless Greg must have felt at the time.

Amanda reached out to her mother both for comfort and to offer comfort to her, but nothing was getting through the pain Jenny felt, nothing at all. Amanda turned to God, her husband, Ross, and her little girl, Beth. Ross was wonderful during her time of need. Often he would hold Amanda in his arms and pray with and for her. He was a wonderful man and throughout this entire ordeal, he was supportive to all of them. He stepped in to help Greg during this time also, because he could see Jenny couldn't.

Jenny can barely remember the funeral. The days turned into weeks, the weeks into months, and Jenny found no peace. None of this made any sense. She couldn't accept the police accounts of Bret's death. He was happy. He was fine. Bret had everything to live for. There was no note, there were no witnesses and absolutely no reason for him to have done this. Jenny could remember thinking surely this had to be murder. Denial and her sense of loss were all encompassing in her life and Jenny withdrew from life. Nothing seemed to matter to her any more. She lost contact with her husband and family. She lost hope and any degree of reality. But worse than this, she lost her connection to God. It was as if she blamed Him for Bret's death.

She didn't see Greg's needs or pain. He tried desperately to get through to Jenny. He wanted to help her, but he also needed her to help him deal with the horrific loss. Amanda tried desperately and repeatedly to reach her mother, but there was no getting through. Eight months after Bret's death, Greg packed his clothes and moved out of the house. He wasn't leaving Jenny so much as, he too, crumbled under the weight of the loss of his son, as well as the loss of his life as he once knew it. Looking back on it now, Jenny believed Greg honestly tried, but at that point in time, nothing seemed to matter. Jenny has fallen so deeply into her own depression and grief, only a miracle could have helped her.

Jenny remembers waking up one morning about ten months after Bret died, and almost two months after Greg left their home, to a little tap-tap-tap at the bedroom door. As she looked over the covers she saw little Beth come running into the bedroom. Her eyes were so wide and she was so excited. "Grandma, Mommy is making us pancakes with real strawberries! We get to eat them up in your bed", she said with her little arms reaching out for grandma to help her into bed. Jenny reached out and pulled Beth up, and tucked her under the covers. For the first time in almost ten months, Jenny felt something other than pain. With her granddaughter tucked in her bed and in her arms, she felt comforted and for the first time in a very long time, she even felt loved.

Amanda came into the room with a breakfast tray to find Jenny and Beth giggling about Beth's cold little baby feet. Amanda poured two cups of coffee and handed one to her mother. Then she gave Beth a cup of hot chocolate. "This will warm you up," she said, "inside and out. Beth honey, will you say a prayer before we eat our pancakes?"

Beth put her cup back on the tray, folded her little hands and bowed her head and prayed, "Please, Jesus, bless this food. Thank you for making Grandma smile, again. I love you, Jesus. Amen". Jenny looked up and saw tears in her daughter's eyes and for the first time since Bret's death she saw the devastation and the loss Amanda must have felt all of these many months. She not only lost her brother tragically, but she also lost her mom. Jenny realized for the first time how selfish she had been. All of them lost Bret, not just her. How could she have abandoned her daughter like that? What was she thinking? And Greg, what had she done to him?

Jenny reached out her arms to hold her daughter and whispered, "Forgive me Amanda, please. Sweet Jesus, please forgive me. I'm so very sorry. Oh Jesus, what have I done? Help me, Lord. Oh my God, please help me." Jenny can remember holding Amanda tighter than she had ever held her before. Both women cried tears of joy.

Beth joined in on the family hug and then asked, "Are we going to eat our pancakes now?" Amanda and Jenny both laughed. The three of them ate the pancakes and, curled up in the bed and, talked for hours. They laughed and cried. They talked about the important things in life. At one point, Beth fell asleep for a while, and Jenny and Amanda talked about Bret. This was the first time Jenny saw the extent of the pain Amanda suffered at the loss of her brother.

Both women were searching for an answer as to why Bret would have done this. There appeared to be no reason for him to have taken such drastic action. No one could answer why he did this. Still the police investigation led to one conclusion, and only one conclusion. Bret killed himself. Amanda suggested that someday when they go to heaven, they might then know the answer. But for now, it was time to get on with their lives. It was time to heal.

This was the first step in the healing process. Jenny knew she had a long way to go, but she also realized she didn't have to go through it alone. She not only had found her way back to her daughter and her granddaughter, but she also made a reconnection to her Father in heaven, Jesus and the Holy Spirit. She recognized the simple fact that she had left all of them. And all this time she needed only to reach out, for they were there waiting to hold her in arms of forgiveness, healing, and love. They were the strength she needed, the power over her grief and the peace she desperately wanted to find.

After Amanda and Beth went home that day, Jenny walked down the hall and stood before the door to Bret's room. She had closed the door the day he died and never went back into it. Where the police or Greg may have gone inside at some point looking for answers during their investigation or to get Bret's suit for burial, she didn't. She just couldn't. Now she knew she must go in as her hand touched the doorknob and she slowly turned it. She wanted to go inside, and at the same time, she didn't want to.

.   Jenny dropped down to her knees and prayed, "My precious heavenly Father, in Jesus name, give me the strength to do what I must do. Lord, help me to be who I should be. Make me whole once again so that I can help others. Forgive my stupidity and give me strength and peace. Lord, I need your help and your guidance. Please, light my way and strengthen my faith. Give me the courage to do what must be done, and the wisdom to know what you want me to do. Lead me, Jesus, I will follow. Amen."

As Jenny got up off her knees, she pushed the door open to Bret's room. Slowly she walked inside. She sat on his bed, and thought back about the good times she had with her son and the rest of her family. This was the room she and Greg first turned into a nursery when they were expecting Amanda. As Amanda grew older, they moved her to a room down the hall, and left the nursery the way it was. When Bret was born, the room was ready and waiting. When he was three, they redecorated it more appropriately for a little boy, and the nursery was gone. Later, as Bret grew older, he fixed the room the way he wanted it. Everywhere she looked in this room, Jenny could see reminders of Bret, who he was, and what was important to him.

A Place to Warm Your Heart
A Trilogy of Hope and Inspirational Poems

As Jenny sat the on his bed, she was surrounded by all of the loving memories of her son that she had locked away somewhere in her heart. He was such a beautiful and loving child and she felt the warmth of his presence around her. As she looked back over the years, even during the bad ones when he was so emotionally and mentally ill, there were many good memories. She recalled how she used to sit on that same bed, and tell Bret stories about Jesus and how He healed and helped people. Bret did so love to hear those stories.

Jenny remembered how, after he was finally on the better medications, Bret was so happy and normal. He was such a wonderful teen. He never got into trouble and always studied hard. He was involved in sports and school plays, and he loved to write. Bret also had many friends, and he knew how to be a good friend to others. He had a gentle and giving nature and often volunteered to help others.

That was where he met Deanna. They both volunteered at the local hospital. Then they were in a couple of the school plays together. He just shined after she came into his life. There was no doubt, Deanna truly made him happy. Suddenly, it occurred to Jenny how profoundly Deanna must have been affected by Bret's death. She wondered who was there for her? Jenny realized she had neglected Deanna, also. In her heart Jenny recognized the fact that Bret would have wanted someone to be there for Deanna. Jenny felt sick at the thought of how miserably she had failed everyone; Greg, Amanda, Beth, Ross, Deanna, Jesus and even herself! "No more," she said, "today, Jesus, I'm going to start living for others. Now, I will do things as He would have me do them."

Just then, Jenny heard a noise coming from the back yard. She walked over to the window and looked out. Greg was in the garden working. She noticed how beautiful the garden looked. She hadn't been out there in what seemed to be forever. Jenny couldn't remember the last time she'd even looked out of the window. It was as if she had gone away for a very long time, and let everything go to ruin. Still the garden looked beautiful, in spite of the fact that she hadn't touched it since Bret's death. Obviously, someone else had.

She wondered, should I go down? Should I go out to help Greg? Maybe he's waiting for me to go out, or maybe he wants to be alone. Jenny wanted to go down, but she just stood there, afraid of how Greg might react to seeing her. Soon, she noticed he was gone. Had she missed her chance? Suddenly everything seemed so complicated. Jenny truly loved Greg and couldn't believe how she could have lost touch with her family to the extent that she had. She wondered if Greg could ever forgive her? Had he gone on with his life and left her behind? How could she have been so foolish?

Just then, the phone rang and Jenny reached over to answer it. It was Amanda. Jenny can remember thinking how nice it was to hear her voice. It seemed she just called to see how Jenny was feeling since she and Beth left her earlier in the day, and to say she loved her. Jenny assured her daughter that she was feeling just fine, and that she loved her, too. Jenny also felt the need to reassure Amanda that everything was going to be all right from now on. Jenny realized she had a long way to go, but at least now she was standing on her feet, moving forward, and thanking God for the chance she had to do so.

As Jenny was going to leave the room, she noticed Bret's favorite sweatshirt lying in the corner of the bedroom floor. She picked it up and opened the closet to hang it. This felt familiar and almost comforting to her. She was always picking up after Bret when he was younger.

As she stood in front of his closet it occurred to her that everything was the way Bret left it, almost like a shrine placed there to honor his memory. But Bret was gone. Keeping things as they once were, wasn't going to bring him back. Jenny took a deep breath and started to take the clothes out of his closet. She folded the pieces neatly and placed each of them on his bed. Soon, all the clothes were neatly folded into piles on the bed. Jenny ran down to the basement to see if she had boxes for Bret's things. She did.

Back up in his room she placed Bret's things she had taken from the closet into the boxes. On the floor of the closet, Jenny noticed a shoebox. As she bent down to pick it up, she leaned on a loose floorboard and one end of it lifted slightly. Jenny had never noticed this before. Reaching down she lifted the loose board out of the way. Beneath the floor, Jenny saw a stack of tablets. Carefully she lifted them out of their hiding place. Each tablet had a number on it and some had a date of beginning and end. She put them in chronological order starting from the one dated farthest back in time to the most recent date. The most recent, was the day before Bret died and was also marked with the highest number.

Jenny was afraid to look, still she knew she had to. She had never seen these tablets before and was unsure of what they were, why they were there, or what to expect. She can remember sitting on the bed just looking at them. Finally, she prayed. Jenny remembered that prayer well. "My Jesus, I have hurt and failed everyone in my life. I want to make things right somehow, but Lord I don't know where to start? I fear what I might find in these pages. Precious Lord, please help me to do this, lead me, show me. Where do I begin?" Suddenly, she knew she must start in the beginning. Slowly she opened the oldest book which was marked Number One. She wondered if in these pages, she would find the answers she desperately needed.

Her hands shaking and tears in her eyes, she opened the first book. The pages were filled with the word "No" written over and over repeatedly. Sometimes in very tiny letters, then in big bold letters. There were some "X's" and scribbling on some of the pages, too. In some of the margins were senseless pieces of gibberish. Not words Jenny could make any sense of. They were more like ramblings, or senseless scribbling. There were a few pictures that looked like knives.

As she held this first tablet, she ran her hand over the pages as if feeling each of them might help to explain what all of this might mean. Jenny could remember feeling close to Bret, almost like a kind of warmth around her, as she sat there in his room reading the things he once wrote.

"Please, Jesus, Help me understand what I need to know. Are you trying to tell me something? Is Bret trying to show me something? Is there something he wants me to know, or do? Please, Lord, help me to understand," Jenny whispered again in prayer. The next two tablets were very similar to the first one. Clearly this didn't make sense to Jenny, but with hope and faith she pressed on.

Taking the forth tablet in her hand, Jenny walked down the stairs and into her kitchen. She set the tablet on the kitchen counter and made a cup of tea. When the tea was ready, she took the tablet and the cup of tea into the living room and sat down on the window seat by the window overlooking the garden. There she opened the forth tablet. Inside this one she saw words and phrases, but again they were repeated over and over. Here Bret had written, "I don't want to hear it -no more -no more. Make it stop. 2 many noises! Help me! Go away! Big hole, go away! Stop it. Stop it! No. No!!" This was repeated both in part, and exactly this same way, throughout this tablet. Also, Jenny noticed as she looked through this one, the handwriting was looking more like Bret's. There were things scribbled in the margins and where she couldn't make out most of them, a couple of them said things like, "I hate me," and "good voices," or "bad voices." Everything was very repetitive and seemed confused, conflictive. She noticed some pages had been torn from the tablet, and she wondered, why?

There, in between the last page of the tablet and the back cover, was a folded piece of paper that looked like one that may have torn out of the tablet. On this page, as she unfolded the paper, there was a picture, which horrified Jenny. On this paper was a picture of a person she thought looked like a child, sitting on a chair, with its head severed from the body, and the head was on the floor. There was a picture of a knife, also on the floor, in a pool of blood. The picture itself had been crossed out with a big X over it, but Jenny could clearly see it. Where everything up to this point in the tablets was disturbing, it wasn't horrifying like this picture. This picture made her feel physically ill. Seeing this was very upsetting to Jenny. She wanted to know the truth, and for the first time, was beginning to realize the truth was awful.

As Jenny finished this tablet she ran upstairs to get the stack of the rest of the them. She felt as if she was beginning to see a pattern emerge. Could this be a journal of sorts of Bret's feelings and tortured mind? A kind of documentation of his illness as he saw it or lived it. She wasn't sure, but she knew she had to follow this to the end no matter where it may lead her. The picture was awful! Now she wished she had finished college. Maybe these things would make more sense to her now if she had been better educated before. She wondered if, maybe she could have done more to help her son back when he was in this kind of pain, if she'd been trained to recognize it? Would more knowledge have helped? Jenny couldn't help but wonder.

In the next tablet, he had written pages of, "I hate me," over and over again. "Stay away from the dark hole," resounded throughout the pages as well as, "don't listen to bad voices," echoing warnings of darkness. Jenny cried at the thought that her son had fallen so far away from reality and was being tortured so horribly in his own mind. How he must have suffered! He was still a young child when he wrote this and drew the picture. Jenny thought about the many doctors Bret had seen, and the all times she and Greg took Bret in to see them seeking help and answers. Now, here lay his legacy in black and white on tear stained pages. First Bret's tears, and now Jenny's.

"I don't want to hear it - no more - no more. Make it stop. Don't listen to bad voices," continued through the next two tablets. Nothing positive, only more of the same. Jenny's tears fell on those of her son. The emptiness in her heart was incredible. Nothing in her life could have prepared her for this kind of pain. Nothing. As she went into the next tablet she had to touch each page, running her hands across each word, as if to somehow communicate with her son, wanting to understand his pain, needing to feel his sorrow, wanting to stop, yet knowing she couldn't. Jenny made herself go forward. This really hurt. Jenny never knew how far from reality her son had fallen. Agonizing over his every word, she began to see that this pain and fear *was* Bret's reality. This fact made her feel as if she would choke on that aching lump that had grown in her throat.

Opening the seventh book, Jenny finally saw the first positive thing. There, on the second page was a heart he had drawn and inside, Bret had written, "I love you." Nothing more, just I love you.

Jenny gasped. This was the first sight of hope she felt since Bret died. In this documentation of his horror, she finally saw a glimmer of hope. "Thank you, Jesus," she whispered as she anxiously turned the page. She remembered praying she would see more of this as she went on.

Jenny noticed there were more pages missing after the heart page and again, she wondered why. She knew pages were torn out, because some remnants of the torn pages remained in the binding of the tablet. She wondered what was on those pages and why Bret might have removed them. She hoped all the other removed pages, weren't all like the picture she found folded in the back of one of the earlier tablets. Again, she pressed onward, hoping to see more good things, and less bad.

There were several pages of gibberish and things repeated as they were from the other tablets, but here she also found other things. Even sentences. Well, at least some. "Won ball game today," Bret wrote. Also, he continued, "Saw Pete today, he thinks I'm better. I wonder? Maybe he's right." Jenny remembered Pete was one psychologist Bret saw for quite a while. He was the one who put Bret on the medication that helped him the most. Pete had been his doctor for the last six of Bret's final seven years on this earth. Yes, Jenny could see this was also Bret's first sign of hope. She felt it.

Now the tablets took on new meaning to Jenny. She could see Bret was making progress. She remembers wishing she could have found these tablets back when Bret was writing them. Maybe if she had, they could have helped. Jenny continued to follow the paper trail into her son's past and toward any insight all of this might bring.

Jenny saw many more positive entries and less and less of the dark difficult things. Bret was improving during this time in his life. He wrote in the eighth tablet, "Party at Sam's was okay" and "Bad job on math test today. Will have to take make-up." Jenny noticed fewer pages were torn from the tablet now. Was this a good sign? She was unsure, but she felt it might be. One thing Jenny was sure of, Bret seemed to be going through a more positive phase. Aside from an occasional, "I hate me" or "bad voices" scrolled and scribbled into a margin, Bret sounded more like a normal boy in his early teens and less like a tortured soul. Jenny remembered feeling comforted by this at the time.

Bret made entries less at some times and more at others according to the dates in the tablets, but it was as if his busy schedule was more the reason for this than anything else. He commented about his friends, teachers, and family in the ninth and tenth tablets. Most comments were normal things any teen might put into his or her diary. Jenny did see some things she felt were special to her; little things she remembered, too. This felt comforting to her.

Among them were notes Bret made about believing in Jesus. He wrote, "Today I know Jesus lives within me. Mom always tells me this. Today I believe. I was depressed and I prayed. Jesus made me feel better. Darkness can not own me. I am free." Another entry in the eleventh tablet said, "As I face my demons, I do not walk alone. Jesus is with me. Together, we fight the good fight." Jenny was comforted by the fact that Bret was in touch with Jesus in his soul. She found peace in that fact. She remembered thinking if the tablets hold no other answers, finding this fact has made going through all of them well worth the pain and effort. The next three tablets continued in this same way.

As Jenny got into the fifteenth tablet, she began to see signs of depression. The changes in his writing were gradual and Jenny wondered if any teen might feel all these same things? Again, she wondered if she were more educated on this subject, if perhaps, she might know the answer.

Bret made comments about being tired of school, sick of spending his time doing useless homework, and not wanting to do the household chores he had been assigned. He stated he felt tired and didn't want to help Dad with the gardening all the time. Jenny wondered if this was depression, or the thoughts of a typical teenager? Amanda had gone through a phase like this, also. Was that all this was?

Moving into the next tablet, she found it held some of the answers. Even to Jenny's uneducated eye, the truth was evident. When she opened this tablet, her heart sank. She felt sick in the pit of her stomach, tears flowed from her eyes, and her heart ached with pain. Pain, much like the pain she felt when she first heard Bret was dead. She wasn't prepared for this, but then, how could she be? How could any parent see this and not die a little inside?

On the first page of this tablet she read, "Who shall I be today? Bret the good son or... When I put on my clothes should I pull up my disguise with the happy face. Everyone needs to see the happy face; or maybe I should be *what* I am. Evil! Hurting, me and everyone around me. Hurting." Bret continued, "Lies, lies and more lies. Nothing is fine. I want to go away. Hide me somewhere. I should have been an actor. I act very well. I would have been great. I deserve an Oscar for this performance. No one knows the truth. I have nothing to live for here, and yet, no one can see it. I can't let this thing beat me. I must win. I have to win. If only I could be sure I'm supposed to win, maybe I could find the light at the end of the tunnel. Sometimes, I wonder, if I even want to anymore."

Bret rambled for pages about the pain inside himself, and how much he hated it. He made references to death, such as, "To find peace I must die. Only through death, will I be safe from the darkness," and "I pray God will take me. Everyone would be better off if I were gone. I don't want to be here any more. If I died, the noise would stop in my head. Oh God, please stop the noises!"

As Jenny read, she came face to face with Bret's demons in a way she hadn't until now. He had written, "The noises in my head are louder today than yesterday. God, Please make them go away. STATIC POUNDING IN MY HEAD *LOUDER* AND **LOUDER**! No more, please, no more!" The pain continued, and with each page Jenny turned, she saw more of what her son had lived with, and through. Bret went on about the fear he had about right and wrong. He said, "I don't want to hurt anyone. Good voices tell me to find peace. Bad voices want revenge. Punish them!!! Make them pay!!! No head, no problem. Simple. Do it. Do it!" Pages torn from this tablet were many. Almost every other one was torn from the binding. Jenny kept wondering, why? Yet, fearing she already knew the answer.

Jenny asked herself, "Were they so horrible, even he couldn't stand to look at these pages himself?" Tearfully Jenny took the final tablet into her hands. This was the 17th tablet. She held it against her heart, and she prayed, "Jesus, in your name I pray, Lord, help me. My Father in heaven, please, lead me and give me strength. I have feared from the day Bret died that he was condemned to hell for his suicide. This, Jesus, has been my fear and horror. I have lost my son, I have lost my husband, and I fear I will loose my mind. Help me. Please, Jesus, help me. Lead me to a place of peace. I'm too weak to make this journey alone and I need you. Oh Father, don't turn away from me. Forgive my weakness and give me strength. I believe you can. I have faith you will.

In Jesus name, guide my steps, Lord. Light my way. I have to know, Jesus. I have to know. Amen"

Jenny wiped the tears from her eyes and took a deep breath. She knew this was the last tablet and she was still reeling from the horror of the last one she held in her hands. Both fearing, and anticipating this final journal penned by her dead son, she opened the tablet. Inside, she saw only blank pages. As she turned the pages from one to the next, she could barely breathe. Nothing. Nothing! Her heart sank. Trying to catch her breath, Jenny, jumped to her feet. As she stood up, an envelope fell from the last tablet. She picked it up off the floor and clutched it to her breast and sobbed uncontrollably. "Oh, thank you, Jesus. Thank you Jesus. Oh, God, please, please…"

Trying to compose herself, Jenny's trembling hands opened the envelope letting it drop to the floor. She desperately wanted to read what was written on the pages contained within, but the tears flooding her eyes made it impossible to do so. She took a deep breath. Then a couple more and wiped her face. She remembered thinking Jesus has always been with her and with a final deep breath, Jenny felt the presence of peace encompass her soul. "Okay" she said, "I can do this. Thank you, Jesus. We will do this together."

Jenny took a sip of her tea. It was cold. She had been sitting there for hours now, but this was the first time she had given any thought to time since she found the tablets. Now she was nearing the end of this journey through her son's journal of his life, and the sun was setting in the sky. As Jenny stood with pages clutched tightly in her hand, she looked down at the envelope she had discarded in an effort to reach its contents.

Jenny bent down to pick it up, and on the front of the envelope the word *Mom* had been printed. Jenny set the pages of the letter on the window seat along with the envelope and took her cup of cold tea to the kitchen. Heating the water for another cup of tea, Jenny thought about how much she loved her son. The urgency and anxiety she felt a while ago were now gone. She felt relaxed and at peace. The teakettle signaled the water was hot by its familiar whistle, so she made her tea, took it to the living room, and sat down on the window seat. She set the teacup on the little coaster she keeps there for this purpose and curled up to finish what she started hours earlier that day. Jenny took a sip of tea, a deep breath, and took the papers off the seat and held them. There was a rubber band holding them together. There was one page on the top marked "Mom". Jenny pulled it out first and she read:

Mom,

I love you. You have been the best of everything I have known in my life. You never gave up on me, even when I gave up on myself. Thank you for your love. Please read each of these letters first, and then give them to Dad, Amanda and Deanna, as I have addressed them.

The letter I have written to Jesus, I want you to read last. I will leave it in your capable and loving hands. Jesus needs no letter, for I know when I reach out to Him in prayer, it is with love He answers. I need you to know what is in my heart and soul. I need you to feel the comfort, I know this will give you. If you choose to share it with anyone else, you may. I will leave this up to you. Read it with the love I am sending you. I believe you will know what you must do with it. Pray and allow Jesus to lead you. He will know when the time is right. I know this is so. I know it the same way that I knew, you will be the one to find the journal of my pain, and by reading that journal you would be led to these letters.

One day, maybe you and I can help someone else together. I love you today. I will always love you. I will be with you always in Spirit. Mom, forgive me for leaving you this way. Please know I have gone home. I am at peace. My Spirit is now one with Jesus. I am free...

All my love forever,
Bret

Jenny cried, "Oh, my baby, my son. I love you so very much. I always will. I love you, Bret. I love you." Tears caressed the paper her son once touched, and she reached out her arms as if to hold him, then pulling back toward her, cradling the page next to her heart as if to draw him into her soul. "I forgive you Bret," she whispered. "God, please forgive my baby. Let him be with you in heaven. Please, Jesus, forgive him," she sobbed.

Finally composing herself, Jenny looked down at the letters remaining to be read. Next she opened the letter addressed to Deanna thinking this would pull less at her heart than the others. As she read her son's words to this girl he knew for only such a short time, she understood how much Bret had loved and needed her. She read:

My Darling Deanna,

Forgive me for leaving you this way. I love you. I held heaven in my heart and soul when I held you in my arms. I leave you, because I love you. I know you would stand beside me and fight my demons, but Deanna, this is my fight and I could not bare to see you go through this, not with me, or with any children we might have had.

No. I choose to leave you softly, going gently into the night. I go to protect you and the children we might have had. God forbid, I would pass this horror onto someone else. God forbid, another child would be born with this affliction.

Go on with your life. Live it to the fullest. Take from it, everything you can. Find peace, joy and happiness. Be happy, Deanna. Do this for me. Go to college and get your degree. Have that family we talked about. Make a life for yourself.

I will love you forever. You will forever be a part of me. Remember me with love, tenderness, kindness and forgiveness. I go, loving you always.

Bret

Jenny had no idea that Bret and Deanna had become so close. She knew they were in love, well, the way kids fall in love any way. But she never knew he loved her so deeply, or that she had made this profound impact on his life. Now, Jenny could see, this was not simply a crush, puppy love or even the going steady kind of relationship she thought it was. Her son honestly loved this girl.

As she sat looking at this letter, Jenny felt comfort, knowing Bret had felt that kind of love and bond in his life. She owed this girl so much and never really even knew her. Where Bret had brought her home for dinner a couple of times, he never indicated to Jenny, how very special she was to him. Now she was wishing she would have known this, as she sat on the window seat reflecting on the past.

She could remember feeling how much he must have loved Deanna, and how very much he left behind when he walked away from her for the last time, knowing this good-bye was to be the last one. This must have been the most difficult thing he ever had to do. The ache in Jenny's throat and the pain in her heart were overwhelming as she thought of how difficult this must have been for her son.

He spoke of children. He wanted to have children. Now, for the first time, Jenny understood his fear of passing his illness on to his children. She recognized his fear of handing this affliction to Deanna through their children and that she might have to watch her children suffer. He couldn't do that. Not to her, not to a child, and not to himself.

Jenny put the letter down and in her heart, promised Bret to give it to Deanna. She wasn't sure where Deanna was now. Time had passed and Jenny hadn't been there for her. She wondered if Deanna would even talk to her after all this time, but she knew she had to try. This letter belonged to her and Jenny was bound and determined that she should have it. This was what Bret wanted, and Jenny was going to do exactly what Bret requested. Tomorrow this would be her first order of business. But tonight, Jenny still had unfinished business to do.

There were three more letters for her to read. Each of them as important to her as the last two letters. Where it was difficult for Jenny to read and relive all of these things, she knew in her heart, she had to. With every letter, Jenny knew she was coming closer to the truth, the whole truth. Praying with each step she took, Jenny pressed onward.

Taking the letter marked for Amanda, Jenny took a deep breath and opened it. Inside the letter was a little gold bracelet. There was an angel charm on it. This was a very delicate and lovely piece Jenny had never seen before. Jenny turned her attention to the letter and read:

Amanda,

You have been my big sister, my confidant and best friend. I love you. You helped me through things only we know and you have never let me down. I thank you for that. I love you for that and so much more.

I know leaving like this puts a burden on you, but I have to go. If I were to stay, I knew in time I would lose control, and ultimately, lose the battle. I have to leave while my soul is still mine to give to my Savior. Forgive me, please.

I love you. I love Beth Ann with all my heart. I bought this little gift for you to give to her some day when she's old enough to have it. Until then, you wear it and take care of it for her. Remember you have an angel watching over your life now.

Tell Ross to take care of all of you for me. He is a wonderful person and will be with you through anything you may face in the future. Take care of one another. Tell Ross I love him. Ask him to forgive me for leaving him to pick up the pieces.

Take care of Mom and Dad. Forgive my weakness. Always know I love you. See you in heaven, Sis.

I love you,

Bret

Jenny put the little bracelet back into the letter and folded it up. She knew this was a treasure Amanda would hold dear throughout her life. If there is any justice in life, Jenny felt surely, Bret must be in heaven. Truly this much love must be of God.

Beth Ann was very special to Bret. Jenny recognized his need to leave something of himself to her. She knew this bracelet would be treasured Amanda and Beth Ann. He loved both of them deeply.

Next she opened the letter addressed to Dad. With each letter, Jenny understood more of the puzzle, which were the pieces of her son's troubled life. She was trying to put together all of the pieces, in an effort to see the whole picture. When all of the pieces were in place, would see have all of the answers? This was something Jenny wanted to know, as she looked down and read:

Dad,

You are strong, good and kind. You have been a wonderful father and I wish I could have been just like you. If I could take the bad stuff out of me and keep the good and stay, I would. I can't. I've tried and failed. God knows I have. I can't pretend any longer. I'm afraid if I stay, I will hurt those around me. I must leave before the devil owns my soul.

I fight the urge to hurt others around me with every day I spend on this earth. The pills help sometimes, but not enough. If I lose control, someone else might suffer for my weakness. It's bad enough, I must live with my demons, and I don't want all of you to suffer because of them. If I hurt someone, I couldn't live with myself.

Also, if I stay, I will want a marriage like you and Mom have. I know in my heart, this can never be. I would destroy the love my wife would give me, and I fear I might destroy her, also. I would want children. If I passed my affliction to any of them, I couldn't bare it. Even if I adopted a child, I would worry what if I lost control and hurt that child? Could any of us live with that? I know I could not.

I'm sorry for not being able to stick around to help you with the garden as you get older and those old bones ache. I know I should be there to help you. You were always there for me. But you see I have to go away. I don't want to leave, not really. It's just I can't stay and fight anymore. I fear all of you will all be hurt in my battle, between what I know is right and really want, and the demons that haunt me and are trying to overtake my soul.

All of you deserve better than that. I am not depressed here. Things are very clear in my head and in my heart, as I write this. I am looking forward to finding peace with Jesus. There is no peace on this earth for me. Dad, I am so tired. I know Jesus is waiting for me and I pray He will forgive my weakness.

Watch over Deanna for me. I want her to be happy and have a family someday. I want her to fall in love with a man who will love and take care of her. I know she will be fine in time, but for the first months I'm gone, please help her. Take care of Mom and Amanda, too. Forgive me for the pain I know this will bring all of you. I know in my soul, this is better than what might have been if I stayed.

I love you, Dad. Thank you for loving me. I'm sorry I put you through the hard times. Forgive me for all of that, and for what I must do now. Loving you always. It is out of love that I go.

Bret

Jenny wept over the letter to her husband. How would Greg feel about the things this letter reveals? How will all of them feel, for that matter? Bret was tortured beyond any of their fears, and now, Jenny knew how tortured he truly was. She wanted answers about why Bret died and now she had them. She was unsure of how she felt herself about all of this. Even though she has heard, "The truth shall set you free," Jenny wondered, just how does one handle this truth?

Before her lay one more letter. This one was marked simply, "Jesus". Unsure of why Bret might choose to write this letter instead of just praying and talking directly to Jesus, Jenny didn't know. She hoped the answer would lie in the letter itself, as she began to read:

Precious Jesus,

I come to ask you to walk with me through this darkness. Lord, I fear I may hurt another living being. I beg your forgiveness for my thoughts. I have torn from the pages of my life's story, the evil things I have both thought and felt, for even I can not bare to look at them. I know you would forgive me anything. I have read this in your Bible and I believe. But Jesus, I would not be able to forgive myself, if those things jumped off the paper and into reality. Please, Lord, understand, I must keep others safe from me, at any cost.

If I were a stronger man, maybe I could fight this monster that stalks my soul. I feel as if I'm drowning. I live in fear of the pain I could cause others, if I should lose control and hurt someone. I don't want that to happen. Jesus, I have tried to free my mind from these evil thoughts and feelings, and I have failed. The medicine helps me control my actions, but only to a point. If not for your help, Lord, I would have long ago, lost all control and acted on my impulses.

Now, I stand before you, asking you to help me find the strength to protect others. I know you have power over all things, for you can do anything. I am flesh and blood, and the flesh is weak. I know I have a soul, for I have felt you touch it, and you have been my hope. Jesus, I give my soul to you, willingly and with love, knowing you have always loved me, especially when I couldn't love myself.

It is my desire to protect those around me. It is that desire, which brings me to this. And now, Jesus, I reach out, knowing you have seen my demons and recognize them for what they are. Lord, please help me. With your love, I can win. From heaven I could be an angel of light, sent to help another child who is burdened by this pain. Let me be the good voice calling out to a child. With your help, maybe I can finally win this war that rages within me.

If there has been some purpose for me to have lived in this world, Jesus, let it be that in some way, I will have been able to have helped someone else. If you can take from my life anything that might make sense of this madness I have lived, do so. Show this affliction for what it is, Lord. Please allow my life to have meant something. Maybe then, my life will have served a greater purpose.

No more secrets, no more lies. No more being pulled into this pain and fear that has been my life. Jesus, with you I will have peace. With you, I won't fail or be caught in the tempter's snare. I will be free, finally and completely, totally, forever.

My Heavenly Father,

In the name of my Savior, Jesus Christ, I ask forgiveness for my sins of thought, word and deed. I pray you will grant me peace and take my soul, even though I do this thing. Father, touch me with your grace and tender mercies. I commend my soul to you. It is out of love for you Lord, that I now come.

Amen.

Jenny bowed her head and prayed, "In Jesus name, please give my son peace. Lord, show me what I must do and I will follow. Forgive me for not seeing Bret's pain. I want to help other children who cannot help themselves. Teach me, Lord, show me. Amen."

Shaking from the experience of the last fifteen hours, Jenny climbed the stairs and to went bed. As she lay down, exhausted and trembling, with a breathless whisper, she said "Thank you, Jesus." And with that, Jenny drifted off to sleep.

It was almost noon the next morning when Jenny awoke to the sound of her doorbell. Still dressed in the same clothes she had worn the day before, Jenny ran down to see who was at the door. When she opened it, she was both surprised and amazed. It was Deanna who had woken her. Jenny threw her arms around Deanna and gave her a hug.

"Amanda said she thought you were feeling better, and I thought I'd stop in to say hello," Deanna said awkwardly, obviously surprised by Jenny's reaction to her unannounced visit. "Are you, okay?"

"Oh, I'm sorry, Deanna. I haven't seen you for such a long time. How are you? What have you been doing? I was going to call you today," Jenny blurted out. "Come in, Deanna. I'll make breakfast,"

As they passed the mirror in the entry of the house, Jenny caught a glimpse of her own reflection and for the first time realized she was a mess. She had just crawled out of bed, and it showed. Unsure of what Deanna must have been thinking, Jenny hastily put the teakettle on the stove and excused herself to go upstairs and change. A few minutes later, Jenny returned, dressed and combed.

Jenny remembers that afternoon with tenderness. She and Deanna had something to eat and then went into the living room. They talked for hours. Deanna told her she had been in college and was going to work in town for the summer. She said she had missed Bret and was trying to make the best of a bad situation, but it was hard.

Jenny told Deanna how sorry she was for her lack of communication over the many months since Bret died. Deanna was so very sweet and kind and understanding. It was evident to Jenny why Bret loved her. As they talked, Jenny told Deanna about the previous day and about the letters. She showed Deanna the letters addressed to Mom, Deanna and Jesus. They read them together. They both cried as they read the three letters, but then they started to talk about the good things they had in common. They talked about their faith in God and their love for Bret. They each told the other stories about Bret and things each of them knew about who he was, how special their relationships with him were, and how much they loved him.

By the time Deanna left that evening, she and Jenny had become very close. Neither of them knew at that time how close they would become in the future. Jenny just knew that Deanna was a beautiful person, and she felt privileged to count her among her friends.

The next morning Amanda called and invited Jenny to go with her, Ross, and Beth up to their cabin on the weekend. Jenny was unsure about taking the trip up there, and she told Amanda that she wasn't certain about going. She asked Amanda if they could get together to talk for a while and that there was something she wanted Amanda to see. They agreed to meet for lunch.

This was a big step of Jenny. She hadn't left the house since Bret's funeral and she felt a little apprehensive about going out in public again. But deep in her heart, Jenny knew she must move forward. She dressed, gathered Bret's letters, and then went to meet Amanda.

When Jenny arrived at the restaurant, she saw Amanda sitting at a table in the corner and quickly went over to her and gave her a hug. Her daughter looked lovely. As a matter of fact, Amanda was absolutely glowing. Throughout their lunch, they talked about Jenny joining Amanda's family for the weekend at the cabin. Amanda told her that she and Ross had a really good reason for wanting Jenny to come with them on this particular weekend. Finally Jenny gave in and said she would go. It was obvious, this was important to Amanda.

When they finished lunch, Jenny invited Amanda to go to the park with her. As Jenny drove her car and Amanda followed, they headed toward the north end, which was a very secluded part of the park in a wooded area. Jenny wanted to find a quiet place to talk with Amanda and show her the letters.

After parking both cars in the parking lot, Jenny took an old blanket from the back of her car and spread it on the ground a little way into the woods.

After Amanda and Jenny were seated on the blanket, she explained how she had gone to pack the things in Bret's room and had found the tablets under the floorboard. She told Amanda about some of the things she found in the tablets. Although, not all of it. Jenny didn't want to upset her daughter with all of the bad things, and thought if Amanda wanted to see them some day, she could. But today, the tablets weren't her purpose in meeting with Amanda. The letters were.

Jenny took the letters from her purse and showed them to Amanda. First, she showed her the letter to "Mom". This shocked Amanda. Ten months had passed since Bret's death and *now* the letters were found. Both women couldn't believe no one had found them prior to this time. The police had been through the room during their investigation of Bret's death and didn't find them. How could they have missed this?

Amanda unfolded the letter marked "Mom" and read it quietly. With tears in her eyes, she looked up at her mother and questioned, "Oh Mom, he really did it, didn't he? Why didn't we see this coming? How did this happen? Why didn't we see this coming. Oh, no. No! Why didn't he come to me, Mom? Why?"

Jenny tried to comfort her daughter as they sat on the blanket in the woods. She attempted to explain that her brother was tortured in his mind, and that he managed to hide all of this from everyone. She wanted Amanda to understand this was not her fault. This was no one's fault. None of them could have foreseen the things Bret tried so desperately to conceal from all of them and the rest of the world. Taking the letter addressed to "Amanda", she handed it to her. Jenny hoped this would help her to understand more and maybe bring a little comfort to her.

When Amanda opened the letter, she found the bracelet with the angel charm. Holding it tightly in her hand, Amanda read the letter. Tears streamed down her face as she read the words her brother had written to her. When she looked at the charm, the tiny diamond the angel held in her hand glistened in the sunlight as the rays danced around the leaves of the trees and found their way to the tiny angel. The light made the diamond sparkle and glimmer. It was a tiny diamond, but it gave off an incredible glow as Amanda held it lovingly in her hand.

"Look, Mom, it's so delicate and beautiful. Beth and I will both treasure this, always," Amanda sobbed while holding her mother's hand. "Bret and I had so many little secrets, but he never told me he was in this much pain or that he ever felt any of these things. Why didn't he tell me? Maybe I could have helped him. Why? Mom, why?"

Jenny had no answers for Amanda. Instead, she handed the letter to her that Bret had written to Jesus. Amanda took the letter and tried to read it, but the tears flooded her eyes, and she was unable to see the page opened before her. Jenny took the letter from her daughter and lovingly read it to her. Both women cried and held the other. In Bret's letter to Jesus, he had said it all.

The truth was simple; Bret had taken his own life. No matter what anyone would think or feel about his motive or reasoning, the cold hard fact was, Bret had ended his own life. Nothing in either of their minds and hearts could soften this harsh reality. With the acceptance of this fact, perhaps now they could start to heal form the grief that had overtaken their lives. As Amanda and Jenny sat quietly for a while, holding one another, they began a journey of acceptance of the facts and the realities brought forth by these letters.

Jenny and Amanda talked and cried that afternoon, and slowly, they began to heal. They needed to express what they felt, and they needed to say the words that until now had remained unspoken and completely overwhelmed each of them. Finally they could make sense of something that previously made no sense at all. They could understand the pain Bret lived and knew they had to accept the fact that he did what he did. For the first time, they also began to see why he did what he did. Both of them wished they could have helped him and been able to have done more.

Seeing things from the point of view they now had, Jenny and Amanda knew that somehow, through all of this, they would have to eventually come to a place of peace. There would have to be a quiet resignation of what used to be, what is, and what can no longer be. Each of these women felt closer to the other now, than she had ever felt before. They ended the afternoon with Amanda going home to Ross and Beth, and Jenny driving home to her empty house.

Jenny and Amanda planned to go up to the cabin on the weekend and were both looking forward to doing so. Jenny thought that perhaps, she could use the break from the house and being alone. It was as if she had boarded herself up for the better part of a year, and life just went on without her. Yes, going to the cabin with her daughter's family would be a good thing.

Leaving Amanda that day and driving home, suddenly, Jenny remembered feeling the weight of everything she had lost. What was once a full and productive life, now felt barren and empty. Her only son was gone. An act of suicide had taken him from her. Her husband had left months ago. She realized, he must have needed her terribly, and she wasn't there for him. How shutout and alone he must have felt. Her daughter had to deal with this loss alone also. Everything felt completely overwhelming to Jenny that day as she pulled into her driveway and went into that big, old, empty house. She found her way to the window seat and remembered the events of the past. Still sitting at the window on the window seat, Jenny realized she had been there for hours, remembering and contemplating.

Now Jenny knew she had something important left to be done. She took a large envelope out of the desk drawer and placed a copy of each of the letters Bret had written into the envelope. Somewhere in the haze of the last few days, Jenny had copied the letters so each member of the family could have their own copy. Greg had to be given a copy of each of these letters. He needed to see them.

Jenny took the envelope and walked to the door and then realized, she didn't know where Greg was. Sickened at this thought, she ran to the phone. As she dialed Amanda's number, she prayed someone would be there. Amanda answered the phone, and Jenny breathed a sigh of relief.

"Amanda, do you know where your father is? I need to talk to him," Jenny blurted out.

"Mom, are you all right?" Amanda questioned.

"I'm fine, Honey, I just wanted to find Dad," Jenny stated, hoping Amanda could help her.

The phone was silent for a few seconds that seemed like minutes to Jenny, and then she heard a voice on the other end of the phone that seemed both familiar and distant. "Hello," Greg said tentatively, "are you there? Jen?"

Taking a deep breath, Jenny answered, "Greg, how are you? Are you okay?"

Greg's voice was comforting to Jenny, as he said, "I'm making it I guess. Amanda said she saw you, and she showed me the letter Bret wrote to her. Are you okay? Do you need anything?"

"I have a letter for you," Jenny said, wanting to say more and feeling unsure if she should. Was Greg even going to want to see her, Jenny wondered?

"I'm going out of town for about a week on business, but if it's convenient for you, I can stop on my way through and pick it up. Probably around 7:00 a.m. would work for me," Greg stated.

Jenny wanted to see Greg very much, and she was sure this fact must have been evident to him when she answered, "7:00 a.m. will be fine. I'll make you breakfast if you'd like. Maybe we could talk for a few minutes." Taking a deep breath, Jenny waited for Greg's reply hoping he would say yes.

"Let's make it at 6:30. I have appointments set up for tomorrow," Greg suggested.

Jenny was elated. He didn't say no. Trying not to show how excited she was, Jenny said, "6:30 will be fine. See you tomorrow morning. Good night, Greg."

When Jenny hung up the phone, she felt excited and almost like a teenager who'd just made her first date. She ran up stairs and jumped into the shower and got ready for bed, very much looking forward to the next morning. She set the alarm for 5:00 a.m. so she would have plenty of time to get dressed and make breakfast for her husband.

Jenny found it difficult to sleep. There were so many things running though her mind. She wondered if Greg was looking forward to seeing her as much as she wanted to see him. Had he missed her during their separation? How was he going to take the letters Bret had written? What was she going to make for breakfast? What should she wear?

At 2:30 a.m., Jenny could remember looking at the clock and wondering if this night would ever end. But, then she must have drifted off to sleep because the next thing she remembered was hearing the alarm clock going off. She flew out of bed anxious to face the day. She grabbed her blue sweater out of the closet and a pair of jeans she knew Greg liked her in. She finished dressing and fixed her hair. She was actually nervous. Standing in front of the mirror, she took one last look, took a deep breath, and decided this was about as good as it was going to get.

Down in the kitchen, Jenny made coffee and mixed up a pan of Greg's favorite coffeecake and popped it in the oven. Next, she thought she'd make an omelet. This was Greg's favorite breakfast and she wanted everything to be perfect. She set the table and poured two glasses of juice. She was ready.

Jenny walked into the den where she had placed the envelope she had prepared for Greg. Bringing it out into the kitchen, she wondered how Greg would feel when he read them. She prayed that Jesus would be with both of them this morning.

The doorbell rang, and Jenny ran to get the door. When she opened it, Greg stood there with a smile and a bouquet of flowers. She reached to take them from him, and he gently touched her face and said, "I've missed you Jen."

Unable to stop herself, Jenny threw her arms around Greg's neck and embraced him. "Greg, I'm so sorry. Forgive me. I was so selfish," Jenny sobbed as Greg's arms enfolded around her drawing her near. This was a very brief and tender moment between them.

"Hey, what does a guy have to do to get a little breakfast around here," Greg joked, trying to lighten the mood and put Jenny's mind at ease.

Wiping her eyes, Jenny stepped back and took Greg by the hand and led him to the kitchen where she had breakfast ready to serve. They sat and ate while making small talk mostly. They smiled and laughed a little. Beth Ann felt like a safe area of conversation for both of them, and she became the focal point over their breakfast.

When they'd finished eating, Jenny refilled their coffee cups and suggested they go out into the garden for a few minutes before Greg would have to leave. Taking their coffee and the envelope Jenny had ready for Greg, they went into the garden. This was a very familiar and comforting place, and the garden held wonderful memories for both of them. The weather was beautiful. The birds were singing and the little squirrels and chipmunks were running around. The sun was warm and comforting. It felt very peaceful for both of them out there.

Jenny briefly explained to Greg how and where she found the letters Bret had written. She told him she regretted the past few months and the way she had handled Bret's death. She told Greg she knew she had let him down and prayed he could forgive her.

Greg told Jenny he believed he had let her down. He said he had left the house only because he didn't know what else to do. He explained that since he had to leave soon, it was probably not the best time to go into all of this. With a promise that they would talk when he got back from his trip, Greg took the envelope, told Jenny to enjoy her weekend at the cabin with Amanda, Ross and Beth Ann. Greg kissed Jenny gently, and left.

Jenny sat there in the garden for a while a little unsure of what just happened. She had been hoping for more, but she realized that Greg was really pressed for time, and she decided not to worry about it. With a little prayer, she asked Jesus to keep Greg safe and bring him back to her so she could make things up to him.

A few hours later, Jenny was on her way up to the cabin with Amanda, Ross, and Beth Ann. This was about two-hour drive. Beth Ann kept Jenny busy during the entire trip playing games. After a time they were at the cabin in the woods. It was beautiful up there. The weather was perfect, and it was relaxing and quiet. Jenny knew this was just what she needed. She was wishing Greg could have been there with her, too.

Having time alone with her daughter and her family was long overdue. They spent the day together hiking through the woods and fishing from the dock. After dinner that evening, they built a fire in the fireplace and sat around talking. Jenny enjoyed this time with all of them very much. She missed Greg, but she was content with what she had now.

After Amanda and Ross had tucked Beth into bed and said her prayers with her, Grandma Jenny went in to read her a story. By the time Jenny was half way through the story, Beth Ann was fast asleep. So, Jenny kissed her good night and turned off the light.

When she went back over by the fireplace where Amanda and Ross were sitting, she sat in front of the fire to enjoy watching the flames as they danced across the logs. Amanda was smiling and said, "Mom, you look a little more relaxed tonight. Did you and Dad have a nice visit today? You really haven't mentioned it."

"Yes, we had breakfast and then went out in the garden for a while," Jenny answered, hoping Amanda wouldn't ask her to be any more specific than that.

"Dad has been staying in our spare room since he moved out of the house. I don't think he wanted to do anything permanent for a while. He's been hoping you'd be feeling better soon. Are you feeling better? You seem to be," Amanda said, obviously needing some kind of reassurance.

Jenny was feeling better and wanted both Amanda and Ross to know it, but she was less sure of her position with her husband and didn't want to raise any false hope. "Yes," Jenny stated, "I am feeling better. Dad and I will talk more about things when he gets back into town. I hope he can forgive me, but I guess time will tell. I'm sorry that your lives have been turned up side down because of my problems. I realize I am not the only person who's suffered over the loss of your brother, but I guess it's taken me a while to see past my own grief. This hasn't been fair to any of you. I'm sorry for the pain I know I've caused all of you."

"No, Mom don't apologize. You've been through a lot. We understand completely," Ross said reassuringly to Jenny. "Dad is welcome to stay until the two of you are ready to get back on track and deal with whatever you have to. Anyway, we have time. Well at least a few months."

Jenny questioned, "A few months?"

"Yup. You see, Amanda and I will be needing the spare bedroom for a nursery in about six months," Ross joked, "so, we'll have to send Dad back to you soon. We're not sure if he's going to like having stars and moons hanging from his ceiling."

Jenny couldn't believe it. She was ecstatic! "When, why didn't you tell me? Are you sure? Does Beth know? Does Dad Know? Oh, I'm so happy for you," Jenny rambled on, thrilled at the idea of having another grandchild.

They all laughed and talked about this very good news. Yes, Greg knew. He stumbled over the home pregnancy test kit one day last week. No, Beth Ann didn't know yet. They were afraid she might spoil the surprise Amanda and Ross wanted to keep until this weekend. Jenny felt really good about this. The gift of a new grandchild made her extremely happy and she told them so. It was as if something about her life had taken on new meaning now. Jenny was elated. A new life would bring a new beginning for all of them.

Realizing that Ross and Amanda might like to have a little time alone, Jenny told them she was going to go out for a short walk and get some air. She slipped her jacket on and went out side. It was a beautiful evening. Jenny felt better at that moment than she had felt in a very long time. It was peaceful up there at the cabin, and all of her problems seemed suddenly to be far away from her somehow.

She was going to have another grandchild. This felt so right and so good to her as she walked along the little road and down to the lake. She wondered if the baby would be a boy or a girl? It didn't matter. Jenny felt at peace for the first time in what seemed to be forever. She wondered if Greg was as happy about this as she was. She thought back about how happy he was when their little Beth Ann was born. Yes, he had to be happy, too. This would be something they could both look forward to. Jenny couldn't wait to talk with Greg about this. She knew it was something they could share.

The moon was peaking through a cloud and it helped to illuminate Jenny's path toward the lake. When she got by the lake, she sat on an old log that had been lying there for years. She looked up at the heavens and said a prayer that

Jesus would be with Amanda throughout her pregnancy and that the baby would be healthy and happy. She thanked Jesus for the help He had given her and for His comfort and love. She asked Jesus to help her to find peace and to guide her beyond the grief she once had allowed to overtake her life. She also prayed that Greg would be able to find it in his heart to forgive her, because now she recognized how very much she was missing him.

When she opened her eyes, Jenny saw a bright star shining from the heavens. It was much brighter than any star she had seen before in the sky. Then, she saw a second, and a third stars shining down on her. All three of them were surrounded by a mist-like halo. As she sat on the log looking over the lake, she felt warmth and peace surround her unlike anything she had ever felt before. Then, as if through the misty halo, she felt the presence of her son. It was unmistakable and she called out his name.

"Bret, oh my baby, are you there? Is this really you? Oh, Jesus," Jenny exclaimed breathlessly in amazement, "Bret is with you in heaven, Lord. Thank you, Jesus. Thank you, Jesus!" Jenny reached her hand up toward the heavens and called out to her son, "Bret, I love you." The star in the center of the other two twinkled. Jenny stood transfixed in the sight that Jesus had placed before her and through His magnificent power, allowed her to see and experience. She knew Bret was in heaven with Jesus, our Father and the Holy Spirit. She no longer had any fear that Bret had been lost to darkness and banished from the Kingdom of God. There was no longer any doubt that her son had been saved and was in the arms of Jesus and before the thrown of God. Jenny had never felt this kind of peace, or passion before in her life and this was truly of God. This was the miracle Jenny had prayed for.

She stood there, in the presence of the spirit of her son Bret, her Father in Heaven and her Jesus, basking in the glory of the awesome power of their love.

"Oh Bret," she whispered, "what do you want to tell me? Jesus, please help me to understand. Thank you, for showing me that my son is with you. Bret I love you. I will always love you. Thank you, Jesus." Now, Jenny's tears were tears of joy. All of the fear and pain of the past months were melting into a fading memory, never again to haunt her soul. She was at that moment, one with the Lord and, for the first time in a very long time, truly at peace.

Suddenly something broke her concentration and jolted her back into some degree of reality. Her cell phone was ringing from within her jacket pocket. She fumbled clumsily to retrieve and answer it, if for no other reason, to stop the noise and distraction from what she was feeling.

"Hello," Jenny answered automatically, her mind clearly on something else.

"Jenny, thank God you answered. I had to talk to you," a tearful voice on the other end of the phone cried. "Honey, I read Bret's letters and I needed to hear your voice. I tried to call earlier, but I couldn't get through. Finally I went outside with my cell phone to get better reception, and I saw something I have to share with you. I can't believe what I'm seeing." Greg continued, "There are three stars and I feel like one of them is Bret. Jen, am I loosing my mind? I can feel him here with me. It's as if he is here trying to communicate with me. I must be loosing it!"

"No. No, Greg, I'm standing down by the lake and I see them, too. They have a misty halo around all three of them, and Bret is the one in the middle. I can feel his presence, too," Jenny said, reassuring her husband this was real. "He wants us to know he is in heaven," Jenny continued, "and at peace. Greg, he never wanted to hurt us. He loves us and will always be with us in spirit."

"Bret is really here, isn't he, Jen. Do you feel him, too?" Greg asked, not really needing, or expecting an answer. "He's in heaven, Jen. Our son is in heaven," Greg cried. "Jenny I love you. I need you. I want to be with you. We belong together. I want to come home. Bret never wanted us to be torn apart by his death. I know this now. I believe this with every part of my being," Greg sobbed, pleading with Jenny, explaining how he felt, and praying she would understand.

"Greg, I've missed you, and I need you, too," Jenny cried. "Bret's at peace now, and we have to be, also. I love you with all my heart and soul, and I promise you, I will never leave you again. Greg, I am so sorry for the pain I've caused you. Bret was your only son, too. I was blinded by the pain, and swept away by the grief. I lost sight of everything else in my life. I'm so sorry that I wasn't there for you when you needed me. I love you. Please, forgive me. Can you forgive me, Greg? Pray with me. Please, God is giving us something so very precious right now."

Standing there under the three stars surrounded by the halo of mist, more than nine hundred miles apart, Jenny and Greg bowed their heads in prayer. They spoke from their hearts, thanking Jesus and their Father in heaven for the gift that was their son. They were thankful to have had this wonderful child in their lives, if only for the brief time he lived here on earth. They knew they were blessed. As they prayed, they expressed their unending gratitude for the knowledge that their beloved son was in heaven and at peace. As they ended their prayer with a promise to try to help other children lost in the darkness that had consumed their son, and also to stand together in this goal, they said a united, "Amen."

When they looked up toward heaven again, the stars were gone. Both Jenny and Greg felt at peace with the gift they had been given by God, Jesus, and their son. Their son had bestowed upon them a treasure unparalleled by any other they had ever known. They were unsure if they should ever tell anyone about this event, and they agreed to talk about it more when they could be together in person. Jenny and Greg reunited on the phone that night. They both learned that Bret was in heaven and their unspoken fears were relieved. Their minds were put at ease and they were given peace.

Greg moved back into the house when he returned from his business trip. He and Jenny have built an even stronger marriage and bond of trust than they had before Bret died. Now they tend the garden of life together, hand in hand. They thank God every day for the gift of their love.

Jenny went back to college and got her degree in psychology and is now working with troubled children in an effort to help them. She hopes to keep anyone else from falling into the same darkness that had overtaken her son's life. She believes this is what Jesus wants her to do.

Greg and Jenny have opened their home to troubled children and work together to make a difference in the lives of these children. Both of them believe that this is what Bret would have wanted.

Amanda and Ross had their second child and have a strong, happy marriage. Beth Ann has a beautiful little sister now and takes very good care of her. One day, when Beth Ann is old enough to understand, Amanda plans to tell her about her Uncle Bret and give her the bracelet he bought for her.

Deanna finished college and is an elementary school teacher on the West Coast. She has remained close to Jenny, Greg, and Amanda. She plans to marry a wonderful young man this summer. Bret's family will attend their wedding.

Jenny and Greg still live in the home they bought when they were first married. The garden is even more beautiful now than it was before, because they often work out there with the children that come to stay with them. They realize this garden is only a physical place here on earth and will serve only the purpose they allow it to serve. Spending time in this place together and with the children that come to stay with Jenny and Greg gives all of them a peaceful place to talk. This also offers an opportunity to share quality time with each child. Jenny and Greg realize that the important garden in their lives is the garden of life, and this is the one that must be tended daily, unceasingly, and with the help of God.

His family remembers Bret with love. They are all at peace in their own hearts now, and they believe Bret is in heaven looking down on them and trying in some way to help other children who suffer as he once did. Jenny and Greg believe Bret came to them that night in the form of a star so they would understand God's greater plan and to bring them peace.

Almost five years after Bret committed suicide, Jenny was given a copy of my first book titled *A Place to Warm Your Heart Inspirational Poems and Life Experiences* by a friend. After reading it, she showed the book to Greg. He also read it, and they both felt that perhaps seeing my book was part of the greater plan intended by God.

Jenny felt compelled to contact me and ask if I would consider writing the story of Bret's life and death. She and Greg both believe the reason Bret suffered from his affliction was to call attention to this problem and hopefully to stop another child from having to suffer so silently and in secret. They believe if more is known about this affliction and others like it, lives may be saved and children in this kind of pain can receive the help they need. They pray that Jesus will, through this story, help others.

I prayed about this request and was unsure of my ability to take on a project such as this. As I gathered the information sent to me by Jenny and Greg, I struggled with my own issues in regard to this story and found myself, often on my knees, asking Jesus for help.

Then, one day while I was cleaning through my closet, I came upon some old folders of music I had tucked away. When I went to set them on the dresser, one of the folders fell open and onto the floor. When I picked it up, it was open to a page with a song I had written almost twenty years ago. The song is titled *With Grace and Tender Mercies.* The next day I received copies of the letters Bret had written to his loved ones shortly before he took his own life. Jenny wanted me to have them.

When I read those letters, I realized that Jesus wanted me to include Bret's story and the Song Poem I had composed almost twenty years ago in my next book. This song was written many years before the letters were written by Bret, and were in fact, completed when Bret was just a small child, long before the onset of his mental illness. It was at this point that I agreed to write this story. For I, too, now believe this was a part of God's greater plan.

Bret referred to his demons in his writing. On some level, I believe he recognized them for what they were. I know from personal experience that unclean spirits can invade one's body, and if left there to do so, can reek havoc in one's life. Perhaps if they are recognized for what they are, through fasting and prayer, these demons can be cast from the body and free the person from them.

I also know that physical chemical imbalances in the body can, and do, cause problems for many people. Modern medicine has developed medications that can be very beneficial in the treatment of these imbalances. Also, counseling by a professional may be helpful and needed in some cases. But first, we must recognize a problem exists.

However, we need to keep in mind one very important factor in all of these cases. Jesus can do anything. If we do all things in Jesus name, He will help us and lead us to the best treatment for each of us. We need to ask Him for guidance and reach out to Him in prayer. He knows our every need, and He will help us. Whether we need to cast a demon from someone, get medication for him or her, or place them in the hands of a medical professional, if we include Jesus in our choices, He will lead the way. Trust Him. He loves us and wants us to come to Him. Jesus has power over Satan and his demons. We need to recognize this and use Jesus' great and loving power to help not only ourselves, but also, all of those around us.

If we read in our Bibles, and in Jesus name, ask for understanding and guidance He will show us what to do. He will teach us how to do it. In the seventeenth chapter of Matthew, the verses from about the fourteenth through the twenty-fifth deals with this subject. Open your Bible and read about it for yourself. Knowing this may be very beneficial to you in your own life. Perhaps this knowledge will help someone close to you.

Jesus offers us help in many ways if we will be open to what He wants for us. Pray and ask for guidance, and then listen with your heart. Trust Him to give to you all things you will need. Know that His love is everlasting.

♥ ♥ ♥ ♥ ♥ ♥ ♥

Recently I have been asked, "Do you believe that someone who takes his own life can enter into the Kingdom of Heaven?" If I had been questioned on this topic prior to writing Bret's story, my answer may well have been different than it is now. I now believe that these things are in the hands of God. He makes those decisions, not you or me.

I do not wish to, nor do I believe I should, make these kinds of judgments about someone else's actions and life. I must judge my own actions. The choices each of us might make are completely and totally between our God and ourselves. Each of us must be a judge unto ourselves. What we do, think, or feel is a matter of conscience between each and every one of us, and our God.

I will say this. I personally believe Jenny and Greg saw the three stars and felt the presence of Bret, Jesus Christ, our heavenly Father, and the Holy Spirit. In my own heart I believe that Bret is in heaven. I pray that somehow through his story, Jesus will be able to help others who suffer in their minds, bodies, and souls as Bret did. I am sure that Jesus is the answer to all of these, and any other problems we might face in this life. Thank you Jesus for your gifts of love, grace, forgiveness, and mercy. I pray that in all things, God's will be done.

When you read the Song Poem, *With Grace and Tender Mercies,* keep in mind the fact that I did not know anything about what would happen to Bret when the poem was written. I did not know him or anything about him or his family members. If not for the first book I had written, and Jenny and Greg reading it, I would have never known about these events in their lives, or anything about any of them at all. Surely the Lord moves in mysterious ways. I believe this is an example of one of them.

59

Linda C. Luebke

With Grace and Tender Mercies

Unlike life upon this earth
And far beyond the thing we see,
There is someone who knows us
And all that we might be.

He sees inside our secrets,
He hears unspoken dreams.
He listens to our souls with love,
Lighting the pathway that we seek.

He brushes us with faith, when faith is what we need.
He wipes the past away, with His forgiveness we are clean.
His Spirit folds around us, to protect the soul of man.
He holds us with love in His gracious giving hand.
Now, it is for Him to judge, and it is not for us to say.
It is His will, not ours, that must be done.
Endless compassion is at His command.
He loves us and He knows our every need.
For Jesus touches us
With grace and tender mercies.

Through darkness He will lead,
He understands when we get lost.
With a loving hand it's He
Who guides our way at any cost.

Out of darkness He will lead us,
Holding our soul through anything,
It's true our Father's love will never fade.
He is with us today and for always.

Now, it is for Him to judge, and it is not for us to say.
It is His will, not ours, that must be done.
Endless compassion is at His command.
He loves us and He knows our every need.
For Jesus touches us
With grace and tender mercies.

Jesus, please touch us with grace and tender mercies…

I know that Jesus does not inflict any of us on earth with disease and misfortune. These are things of this world, and He doesn't impose them upon us as punishment, or for any other reason. I do believe that He can and will take these things and, somehow, turn them into a victory for God if we will allow Him to do so.

It is my belief that Jesus wants to help other children who suffer from the problems Bret had. Hopefully through this story Jesus will raise awareness of these kinds illnesses. If we listen to Jesus and to our children, I know we can help those who suffer this kind of pain. There is help for them here on earth through Jesus. We can help them find peace here if we will follow Jesus and allow Him to lead the way. Through Him, there is hope.

Hope Lives On

When all is lost,
And nothing in this world can bring it back.
When there's nothing more that you can do.
Standing empty handed. You face the ugly truth.

And through your pain,
There in the darkest hour before the dawn,
You've searched for a reason to go on,
And have found nothing left to hold onto.

Fearing hope was gone, you reached out to find you're not alone.
As if from out of nowhere, you fall onto your knees,
Crying out, "My Father, please help me, please!"

Then through the mist,
Past hopelessness He reaches out to you,
Like a bolt of lightening from out of the blue,
With a wave of love He rushes over you.

He brings you peace,
With His forgiveness, Jesus makes you clean.
Through His compassion, He draws you close to Him.
Bringing a promise of love, He offers you eternity.

And hope lives on, for you reached out to find you're not alone...

61

As children we may question things we don't understand and we often look to the adults in our lives for the answers. We learn songs like, "Jesus Love's Me", and with innocence and acceptance, we believe. With time, all too often we start to doubt things we once knew and believed in so totally and completely. I believe this is not because we have gained wisdom from our time here on this earth, but rather, because we have forgotten how to communicate with Jesus.

This world has a way of taking away our wonder and innocence. Jesus has a way of giving it back. You see, if we can believe unconditionally in the things of God, we can be as little children again in His eyes. As we search with an open mind and an open heart, Jesus will fill our souls with all of the good things we will need to find our way to heaven.

We will be forgiven as we forgive others. Our faith will be strengthened when we are open to the things of the Lord. We will never walk alone through this world if we will reach out to Jesus. God is love, and His love is unending. It is ours for the asking. We need only to ask and believe.

The bond of family love is very strong and transcends all reason and outside influence. When we accept Jesus as our personal Savior, we are a part of Him, and He becomes a part of us. So too, we are connected to God. There is no power in heaven and on earth that is stronger, nor is there any love that runs deeper. Faith will bring us closer to our Lord if we will ask and believe. Trust Jesus to light the pathway to heaven.

With Nothing More Than Love

I come to you today, my Lord, with nothing more than love.
I have nothing more to offer or to bring.
With faith I reach out lovingly, For it is you who sees my need.
Here in my soul your praises I will sing.

With each step that I take, my Lord, it's you who light my way.
My burdens you will carry up that hill.
When the storms of life rage on, your love will help me carry on.
Through the furry of this world you hold me still.

In quiet contemplation Lord,
I see your strength and so much more.
You forgive my sins, wash and make me clean.
And when my time on earth is through,
Through your loving grace, I'll be with you.
And from heaven with your angels, I will sing...

I look forward to the reward of going to heaven someday. I know I will find peace there which surpasses my capability of understanding. Although I have never personally seen heaven myself, I have spoken to others who have, and by all accounts, I know it is the place I want to spend eternity.

I don't fear death. I know when my body dies, my soul will immediately be in heaven with Jesus. My soul will leave this body and I will go to heaven in the spirit. This body is only temporary and at the end of my time on earth, my soul will rejoice when I am taken to heaven.

We all have souls and spirits. These are the parts of us we need to nurture and fill with the love of God. This is the part of us that will live forever. Someday all of the trials of this world will pass and Jesus will take us home. This will be a day to rejoice in the glory of God.

I was once asked by a girl in her early teens, "How do we know that Jesus is real? How do we know there really is a heaven? Because Jesus isn't sitting here in front of us physically and we can't touch Him or see Him, how do we know that He truly Is? When I was little I was told there is a Santa Clause and an Easter Bunny, and I believed in them too. How can I be sure this isn't the same thing? How do I know God isn't made us to help us get through life?"

I thought about the question for a while, unsure of just how to answer. Finally I asked her, "Do you love your parents, your brother and sister, and your grandparents?"

"Yes, very much," she replied.

"How do you know you love them?" I asked.

"Well, I don't know. I guess it's something I feel," answered the girl.

"You know you love them, because you feel it in your heart. You believe they will help you and be there for you when you need them, because you know they love you, also. You can't see love, touch it, or hold it in your hand, but it is real, isn't it? Can't you feel it?" I asked.

"Yes, I do feel love," she stated, "and I know it exists. Love is real."

Trying to make her understand I said, "Did you know that God is love? He created love. He loves you. Open your mind and heart to this fact, and you will feel Him in your soul. God is love. Love dwells in us if we want it to."

It was at that point that I opened a folder of music I had written several years prior to having that conversation with this young girl and I handed her the following Song Poem.

She sat quietly reading it for a while, and when she finished, she looked up at me and smiled saying, "God must be pretty smart. He had you write the answer to my question before I asked it. He must really know me."

This is the poem I handed her to read.

Linda C. Luebke

If Seeing Is Believing

If seeing is believing and we believed only what we could see,
So many things in heaven and on earth,
Lord, would be lost for me.
Some ask, "If we can't see love and can't hold it in your hand,
Or if we can't touch it or hear it, Jesus,
How are we to understand"?
They've heard there is a heaven, but all they can see is sky.
So what would be the reason to believe,
Not question, "Why?"

Haven't you seen the power of love
In the eyes of a mother with a new born babe?
Or felt your heart break at the loss of a loved one
When you heard they passed away?
If love didn't exist, how could it overwhelm our very soul?
Can you see love? Can you touch love?
Can't you feel it? Don't you Know?

I know there is an answer, Lord,
With power beyond our comprehension.
Your love sweeps across our souls in a spiritual dimension.
If seeing is believing; if I'd believe, I'll see the light.
With faith, trust and understanding
God breathes hope into my life.

So, if you ever doubt it, or question that God lives.
Take comfort in the truth that
Through the Spirit, Jesus *is*...
Step out on faith believing,
He'll touch your soul. He'll ease your mind.
His presence will surround you and lead you to His light.

Haven't you seen the power of love
In the eyes of a mother with a new born babe?
Or felt your heart break at the loss of a loved one
When you heard they passed away?
If love didn't exist, how could it overwhelm our very soul?
Can you see love? Can you touch love?
Can't you feel it? Don't you know...

Most of us experience a reconnection with God over the Christmas Holiday. Being reminded about the birth of Christ is a heart warm and loving experience for most of us. I think it's important to keep in mind throughout the entire year the reason Jesus came here in the first place, and not just on Christmas morning.

Not Just On Christmas Morning

A long time ago in a town named Bethlehem,
Our Father sent His Son to us, to save the souls of man.
For there in a manger with only straw to pad His bed,
Lay a tiny King who'd carry the woes of this world upon His head.

As a star sent from above gathered shepherds, wise men, kings,
No one could truly know the power of the gift this child brings.
And from the heavens far above, looking on this meager place,
A host of angles sang the praises of our Jesus' quiet grace.

Out of love, God sent His Son to us to touch the souls of man.
To teach, lead and guide us so that we might understand.
This gift He sent us willingly, His Son, His Love adorning,
To free us all from death and fear that frosty Christmas morning.

As Jesus grew, so many followed. Some began to fear.
For He healed the sick, raised the dead, taught love to all who'd hear.
As the power of His gentleness drew many more to Him,
Those who feared His gift of love conspired to bring His end.

With a crown of thorns to pierce and adorn our Saviors head,
Upon the cross He carried, they drove nails into His flesh.
The Son of God, this Son of man, our Savior loving and true,
Begged, "Father forgive them, for they know not what they do".

Then, in three days He arose to join His Father on high.
With forgiveness and compassion, He brought life so we won't die.
From His manger; to the cross bore; risen into heavens love adorning,
He brought us all the gift of life, that frosty Christmas morning.

Out of love God sent His Son to us to touch the souls of man.
To teach, lead and guide us so that we might understand.
This gift He sent us willingly, His Son, His Love adorning,
To free us all from death and fear; Not just Christmas morning...

65

God has given us many gifts. Every one of them should be treasured. He understands us. He knows all our human weaknesses. It is He who sees all things, and forgives us with compassion and with grace. He loved us enough to send His only Son to us that we might be saved. This is the greatest gift any of us could have been given.

Coming into the new millennium, many people feared this would be the end of the world. It was not. There have been many other predictions of the end of the world that have also come and passed without event. Some people read in their Bibles, and say they can see the end of the world being predicted within those pages. I believe they are mistaken.

I have read in my Bible and I see something very clearly. The Second Coming of Christ is when He comes to each of us, and when we accept Him as our personal Savior. The Second Coming of Christ is when we give our lives and souls to Jesus, and through baptism in water, symbolically we bury our old lives and then we are risen into our new lives, and are granted everlasting life.

From that point on, each of us becomes a judge unto ourselves. When we do wrong, Jesus will forgive us with compassion and love if we ask Him to. We will make mistakes and bad choices along the way, but through God's gracious and wonderful gift of His only Son, we can be forgiven.

Death has no power over us once we have accepted Jesus into our lives, and eternal life is ours. When our life here on earth is over, our soul shall be immediately with Jesus in heaven. Our body will no longer be needed and will be left here on earth to return to dust. Our souls will rejoice from heaven and we will have everlasting life with Jesus, our Father, and the Holy Spirit.

If we accept Jesus as our personal Savior, and then turn from Him, or chose to do the devils work instead of that of the Lord, our eternity will be spent in hell. Once we have accepted everlasting life, it is ours. Where we chose to spend eternity is up to us.

This is why it is very important to know and understand this. There is no provision in the Bible for accepting Jesus and later rejecting Him. If we make the choice to be with the Lord, we make an eternal commitment.

It is also very important to note here, that with Jesus in our lives here on earth and later in heaven, we will have peace, love, and comfort. There is nothing Jesus will not forgive us, if we are truly repentant and ask forgiveness, and then go on and do better. We will never be alone once we have Jesus in our lives.

These facts are very clear in our Bible. If we will pray and ask for understanding, Jesus will teach each of us the truth. These thing are found in the following places in your Bible: St. John 14:26; Hebrews 9 verses 24 through 28; and in Romans Chapters 6 and 8. Take the time to read these passages, praying first. Allow Jesus to be your teacher.

If I Should Fall

When I was lost,
You were the one to light my way.
You'd guide my path each step I take.
Lord, you held my soul at any cost
To keep it safe from harm.
Jesus, you led me to you
When I was lost.

Lord, you touch me with the strength I need,
When I can't find it on my own.
Stepping out on faith believing;
I know your Spirit will lead me home.

If I should fall,
Lord please be that safe place I can land.
My somewhere to go to find a friend,
The one who'll touch my heart, and then,
Be there with me through it all,
My Jesus, if I should fall.

Jesus, you forgive my weakness
For it's you who sees my soul.
With compassion and forgiveness
Lord, you cleanse and make me whole.

I can find peace,
Lord, in your grace and loving hands.
With compassion you teach me again,
With faith I'll follow and understand.
Jesus, you grant me everything I need.
My Sweet Jesus, with you
I can find peace.

Lord, you touch me with the strength I need
When I can't find it on my own.
Stepping out on faith believing
I know your Spirit will lead me home.

Jesus, please be with me, if I should fall...

67

Linda C. Luebke

Through the Darkest Night

It was a glorious day in mid April as Amy hurried out to her car pushing a cart of groceries. She was pressed for time and moving along quickly and didn't notice a stranger across the parking lot watching her intently. She unloaded the bags of groceries from the cart and into her trunk. Without a thought, she got into her car, buckled her seat belt, and drove out of the parking lot.

Just before going shopping, Amy had dropped her children at school. She had two, Abby, age 14, and Justin, age 11. Having finished the weekly grocery shopping, she was rushing to get everything home and unloaded in an effort to manage to make it to work on time. Looking at her watch, she noticed time was passing much too quickly, and she really needed to hurry.

Amy lived with her husband of 18 years in a quiet residential neighborhood in the suburbs. She and Tom bought a lovely two story home about six years ago, moving out of the city. Both of them believed the suburbs would be a better place to raise their two children. The neighborhood they chose was quiet and well kept.

As Amy pulled up the driveway, her mind was clearly on putting the food away and getting to the bank on time. She had always been a stay at home mom until about four months ago when she decided to take a part time position as a bank teller. Tom was opposed to her taking a job at first, stating they really didn't need the money. But later he realized Amy needed to get out of the house and do something she wanted to do for herself for a change. So, he finally agreed.

Amy's best friend, Terri, had encouraged her to get out of the house and start to build some kind of life away from the kids. She often warned that when they eventually grew up and moved away, the empty nest syndrome might drive her over the edge. Of course, Terri was just joking, but she did have a point.

Anyway, Amy was bored with doing the same old, same old, around the house everyday and wanted to get out a little and spread her wings, so to speak. Ever since Terri had taken a new job herself, she wasn't around much anymore, and this also made Amy feel a little lonely. They used to talk on the phone occasionally, but it seemed they had less and less time to spend together. Taking the job at the bank helped to fill that void in Amy's life.

Amy enjoyed the job very much and was making new friends. Today she was to work a four-hour shift and had to be there by 10:00 a.m. It was 9:20 now as she pulled up the driveway and into the garage. Leaving the garage door open, she grabbed the bags of groceries from the trunk and carried them into the kitchen. Hurriedly she put everything away, ran into the bathroom with an arm full of bathroom supplies she had just bought, and checked her hair in the mirror quickly as she pass in front of it. On her way out, she reached for her purse and raced out the door. Closing the door behind her, Amy flew out of the house and into her car to drive to work. Again, checking the time she noticed it was about 9:40 a.m., and she took a deep breath thinking she would make it to work on time if the traffic would cooperate. Feeling a little more relaxed now, Amy thought about what she needed to do when she arrived at work.

About two blocks from her home, she felt something pushing against the backside of the car seat. Startled, she looked in the mirror. Being panicked, she swerved the car. A man sitting in the seat behind her leaned forward, placed something around her throat, and began to choke her. Tightening the grip on her throat with one hand, he reached forward to steer the car with the other. Amy could barely breathe, and her vision began to blur. She felt as if there were a rock in the pit of her stomach as she tried desperately to loosen the rope-like material the man was using to strangle her. It was too tight. She couldn't get her fingers under it to loosen its grip so she could get some air. Feeling herself slipping away, Amy prayed asking Jesus to forgive her sins, to be with her, and to take her to heaven. No longer in control of her car and gasping for air, Amy began to lose consciousness. Feeling unbearable pain in her throat and in her lungs, Amy felt herself moving away from, and out of, her body. Everything went black...

Amy was a kind and gentle woman who would never intentionally hurt anyone. For the most part she was a trusting soul. As a child she attended church regularly with her parents and she knew about God, although she never really turned her life over to Him. Now, in the seconds before she blacked out, she found herself praying and asking God to forgive her and take her to heaven.

As the darkness closed in around her, Amy felt a warm, comforting peace surrounding her, and then she saw a bright light. It was beckoning her to come, and she felt herself surrender to its powerful peace, serenity, and warmth. She heard a voice calling out to her, soothing her fears, and giving her comfort. As she reached out toward the light with outstretched arms, wanting to draw herself closer, needing to pull her soul into its all encompassing warmth, she felt an overpowering love lift her soul ever closer toward the light and into Jesus' loving embrace. She felt peace and comfort she had never known before.

Amy heard a voice speaking softly, saying, "It is not yet your time to come. You have work still to be done. You must return to do that which I would ask of you. I will send an angel to give you comfort and to guide your way through the darkest night. Know I am with you always. Evil cannot touch your soul if you choose to walk with me. The things of the flesh will pass. The kingdom of God will last forever. Through the darkness, I am with you always. Believe that which I tell you. Have faith in me, for I am the way, the truth and the light. I will dwell within you, and I will comfort you always. Fear not."

Amy knew this was Jesus as she felt Him gently touch her hand. Having never before experienced such a peace or felt such an encompassing love, Amy wanted to stay there with Him; but she understood she must go back. She felt a soft breeze gently lift her, and whisk her away from that place as she felt herself fall back into her body...

Waking, Amy realized she was in a forest. There were trees with light filtering through the leaves, and she could see blurred shadows. The air smelled of moss and had a damp, musty odor where Amy was laying face down on the ground. She was breathing but in severe pain. Her throat hurt every time she tried to swallow. Although she could breath, she would gasp for air trying to get more, needing more, and feeling as if only small amounts would come into her body. She tasted blood and reached up to her mouth trying to feel where the blood was coming from, her nose or her mouth. Everything hurt, and there was blood everywhere. She just didn't know where the blood was coming from, but she was alive, and she could breathe, even though it was difficult to do so. "Oh, Jesus, help me," Amy whispered softly, scarcely able to choke out the words through her pain.

Taking a deeper breath, Amy first tried to sit up, and then she tried to stand. A piercing pain shot through her right arm and shoulder as she tried to lean on it in an effort to get to her feet. The pain was so intense, it took her breath away. Unable to get to her feet, she tried to crawl using her left arm. Her ribs hurt, and her left leg was pounding with pain as she tried to move her body forward. Every inch seemed like a mile as Amy tried to move her battered body.

"Where am I?" Amy screamed through her bruised and aching throat, "Help me! Oh God, please. Someone help me. Where am I? What is this place?" Sobbing, Amy felt pain and fear as she had never before experienced. The light faded into darkness as night fell upon the forest where she lay alone shivering in the dark on the ground in this cold and frightening place.

"Jesus, please be with me," she whispered, as she shivered on the cold ground alone in the night. If sleep overtook her, or if it was Jesus' gentle grace, or perhaps the angel He sent to be with, comfort, and take care of her, who brought her rest, Amy cannot say. She only remembered shivering from the cold, praying, and then drifting off. Through the night she remembered nothing more. Surely, it was through the grace of God that someone watched over her through the night as Amy lay in the forest.

At morning's light, Amy heard some noise that seemed familiar to her. It sounded like vehicles on a highway. She looked around and saw no one. But in a distance, she could hear road noise. Again she tried to stand, but she couldn't. The pain she felt the night before had intensified greatly. Knowing she must reach the road, Amy struggled to move forward.

With her left arm, she pulled her body toward the sounds she believed would lead her to a highway, and hopefully, to some help. As she crawled along the ground, she prayed, begging Jesus to help her and to give her strength. Nearing the end of her endurance, Amy saw light reflecting off a moving vehicle. "Thank you Jesus," she whispered, as she edged her way ever closer to the roadside.

Crawling into the ditch by the roadside, Amy swung her left arm as high as she could in an effort to draw attention to herself as she lay as near the highway as she could get. She heard vehicles passing by on the highway while she lay next to the road in pain. With each approaching vehicle, Amy would create as much movement as possible, praying someone would see her and stop as a seemingly endless number of vehicles drove past.

Finally, she heard the sound of a vehicle stopping and a door slamming. Next, she heard the sound of footsteps coming toward her. Her heart pounded. For the first time since she awoke in the woods, she realized how vulnerable she really was lying there so near to where her assailant had left her to die. Would these footsteps be those of someone wanting to help her, or could they be those of the man who brought her here and left her for dead?

Unsure of what the next moment might bring, Amy took as deep a breath as she could, and she prayed. She remembered the words she heard Jesus say to her about being given an angel, and she prayed this angel was watching over her now. With her heart pounding and feeling as if she were drowning in an ocean of pain, she remembered whispering, "Jesus, please be with me," as she lost consciousness once again...

Remembering bright lights and strange noises as Amy came back into at least some degree of reality, she could hear someone trying to talk to her. This voice was familiar and she was desperately trying to pull herself mentally closer toward the voice. Now, recognizing this was the voice of her husband, Tom, Amy felt tears roll down her face as she tried to reach out her hand toward him.

"Amy, Honey, can your hear me? Oh God, thank you," her husband's voice quivered as he tearfully leaned toward Amy and gently kissed her cheek. He

71

held her hand and reassured her that everything was going to be all right now and that she was safe.

This was the first thing Amy could remember after waking from her two day ordeal. She felt safe and comforted as she lay in a hospital with her husband by her side. She can remember drifting in and out of consciousness for a while, but she felt safe now. She was aware of where she was and she didn't feel threatened.

Several days had passed before Amy was completely coherent and totally aware of her situation. Remembering only bits and pieces of the attack, Amy fought to remember the face of her attacker. Wanting him to be found so she might feel safe again, and also, so he wouldn't hurt anyone else, Amy wanted to help the police as much as she could.

Within three days, Amy was sitting up in bed and starting to feel better. Her right shoulder was broken as was her upper right arm and her wrist. She had four broken ribs and a broken ankle. There were many bruises and abrasions on her body, and she had been beaten about the face and head severely. Bruising on her throat gave evidence of how she had been strangled to unconsciousness, which was the only thing Amy could honestly remember about the attack itself. She was in pain, but she was alive, and in time, she knew she would heal. Emotionally, Amy had been damaged, too. But somehow, she was sure Jesus would help her with that aspect of the healing process. She felt a bond of love and faith in Jesus that she had not possessed prior to the attack. Amy knew He was with her now.

The police came in to talk with Amy in an effort to gather evidence and information so they might find her attacker. But she had little information to give them. She remembered leaving her house headed for work and seeing the man in the back seat of the car, but she never really got a good look at his face before she blacked out from strangulation.

One of the investigators suggested the possibility that hypnosis could help to "jumpstart" Amy's memory, and this might give the authorities something to go on. But Tom was vehemently opposed to this and refused to allow Amy to even consider the possibility of going under hypnosis. Recognizing the fact that Tom was only trying to protect and take care of her, she decided to go along with his decision. Although, she did tell the police as much as she knew, she realized they needed more information to go on than she was able to provide.

Basically, Amy told the investigation team she dropped Abby and Justin at school earlier that morning. Next she drove to the grocery store to do the weekly shopping and then took the groceries home prior to heading for work. She was in a hurry and didn't notice anyone lurking about. She was unable to offer a description of the man who had been hiding in her car. She remembered being strangled and waking up in the forest somewhere. As much as Amy wanted to help the police, she could remember nothing more. It seemed to her, if there were other pieces to this puzzle to be found they would have to find answers on their own.

At that time, the investigators on Amy's case knew only a few things for certain. The police knew that Amy had been found along the highway when an older gentleman who was just passing through on business saw something moving along the side of the road. As he drove closer, he realized it was a woman who had been badly injured. He called the police on his cell phone, and then stayed by Amy's side until the police arrived. He didn't see or hear anything that could help the police.

An investigation was started at that point. From the investigation, these additional facts were discovered. Amy had been strangled, beaten and probably thrown, or jumped from a moving vehicle along the highway. This was determined because Amy had sustained the kinds of injuries that were consistent with someone either jumping or being thrown from a moving vehicle. Officers were able to find some markings on the ground where she had been dragged from the highway to the place she had been taken in the woods. They found some shoe prints in the mud presumably made by the man who dragged Amy into the woods where, according to other physical evidence found in the area, she had been raped. Physical evidence, including DNA found on Amy and in the woods supported this theory and confirmed that Amy had been raped.

When Amy was told about the rape, she felt as if it had happened to someone else. How could she go through all of this and still remember nothing? Three explanations were offered to Amy when she asked why she was unable to remember anything beyond being strangled in the car. The first explanation was that because she had been through so much horror, her mind was repressing the memory of it in order to protect her sanity. The second was that she was, in fact, unconscious during the entire ordeal and therefore would have no real memory of it. The third was that the trauma to her head had caused either permanent or temporary amnesia. In any case, the fact that this had happened to her at all had shaken Amy to her core. She was sickened by the thought of what this monster had done to her.

Still, somewhere in the back of her mind, Amy remembered she had been given an angel to watch over her soul, and she knew Jesus was with her, and He had a greater plan for her life. Unsure of exactly what that plan might be at that point, she decided to hold onto this fact, certain it would likely help her to get through almost anything else she might have to face. After all, she had her family, and her body would heal in time. She knew she had work to be done to help herself get well again, but she felt at peace with the fact that Jesus had something He wanted her to do with her life. This gave her reason to go on. She literally owed her life to Jesus, and from now on, she would follow Him. No matter where that path might lead her, she knew she had to follow Jesus.

One afternoon Amy was resting in the hospital after a particularly difficult therapy session. She was in a great deal of pain when Tom stopped in to see her. He wanted her to know the insurance company had replaced her car with another, and that it was home in the garage ready and waiting when she needed it. Her car had not been found, and the theory was, it probably never would be. The authorities surmised it had most likely been taken to a "chop shop", where it was possibly dismantled and sold for parts as many stolen vehicles often are, or maybe could have been driven far away by now.

Amy had felt some distance between Tom and herself ever since she awoke in the hospital following the attack. He sat with her for a while that day but didn't say much more. Amy told him about almost dying and what she had experienced during the time she was on her way to heaven. Tom stated he thought it was probably just a hallucination. When Amy insisted it was real and said that she knew she had an angel watching over her, Tom made an excuse to leave.

Amy sensed the distance between them widening day by day but felt helpless to do anything to stop it. She wanted to talk with him about the attack and about her feelings about being with Jesus, but he was avoiding those topics, as well as a few others. She had never felt so empty as she was feeling just then. It hurt that he couldn't see how much she needed him. When other people were around, he seemed to be very attentive toward her, but when they were alone, the coolness was obvious.

After Tom had left that day, an elderly lady entered Amy's room asking if she needed anything from the nourishment cart. Amy was upset about Tom's distant behavior, and she felt depressed and disheartened; and apparently it showed.

"Are you sure you won't take something from the nourishment cart, Dear? It might make you feel better," the kindly old woman offered.

"I really don't think you have anything on that cart that will fix what's wrong with me," Amy answered wiping a tear from the side of her face, "but, thank you anyway."

"Oh, so that's how it is. Do you mind if I sit for a while and rest my tired old feet for a minute or two? Ah," sighed the old woman as she kicked her shoes off and melted into the chair in Amy's room. "Now, that's much better. I think you need a different kind of nourishment, my Dear. I've been known to dispense a little soul food from time to time. Is that what you need? Here now," she said in a comforting voice reaching out to touch Amy's hand. "I know you've been through more than most of us have to go through, but you're not alone. Jesus is here and He will listen even when no one else will. Just talk to him, Dear."

As this woman touched Amy's hand, she felt a gentle and warming peace surround her, and she felt comforted, much like she felt the day she was going to heaven. Closing her eyes to savor the moment of inner peace she was experiencing, Amy felt reassured that everything was going to be fine somehow.

Taking a deep breath, Amy whispered, "Thank you, Jesus." When she opened her eyes again, the old woman was gone, along with her shoes and her cart. Amy did feel much better. She thought it a little curious somehow that the old woman left so silently and so quickly without detection, but later thought she might have drifted off to sleep for a while in the comfort of Jesus' loving grace.

Determined to move forward with her life and not allow the rape to destroy her, Amy found herself working hard at her recovery and rehabilitation. Physically, she felt a little better every day, and she was anxious to go home to be with her family. She missed her children terribly and knew she'd feel much better when she could be home with them. She also hoped when she came home that perhaps Tom might feel better, too. Recognizing this had to be difficult for him as well, Amy believed everything would be fine when they got back to a normal life.

While Amy was in the hospital, she was introduced to a rape counselor named Susan, and together, they began working on the issue of getting over the fear of the unidentified man who attacked and raped her. Also, they talked about other issues Amy was going to undergo as a result of the attack. Among them, the HIV testing she would have to have on a regular basis for quite a while, how her husband was handling the situation, and what she should tell her children. Amy began to see there were many other issues stemming from this attack beside the most obvious ones with which she would have to deal.

When Amy told Susan about her visit with Jesus, Susan believed everything Amy told her. Susan said she had heard of other people having similar experiences, although she had never personally experienced it herself. She understood what Amy had been through and believed Jesus would be of great comfort to her through this difficult time in her life. Both women recognized the fact that Amy had a long road ahead of her, but they also believed, with her faith in God, and with the help of this new friendship, Amy was going to be a survivor and not remain a victim. Armed with her faith in God and her angel, Amy moved forward with her life taking one day at a time. With each step, she knew she was that much closer to complete recovery.

Amy's first day back at home from the hospital wasn't quite what she had hoped it would be. Her daughter, Abby, was very quiet and seemed very troubled and unsure of what to say to Amy. There were awkward silences as Abby tried to be helpful while still trying to keep her distance. Amy had never before experienced this kind of behavior from her daughter. It was as if they had become polite strangers somehow, trying to find something in common and safe to talk about. Abby was obviously uncomfortable with the situation and the circumstances she was now being asked to face.

Her son, Justin, kept looking at Amy as if she was going to disappear, or worse yet, drop over dead. He seemed to have a need to be right at her side and would get tears in his eyes every time he'd looked at his mother. Amy was still very bruised and swollen and this was a very visual reminder of what had happened to her. She could see this troubled Justin deeply, and she knew she had to do something. Seeing the pain in his eyes was more than Amy could bear.

Amy wanted to comfort her children and put their minds at ease. However, she was unsure of just what she should do. Finally, as she sat quietly, she prayed, asking Jesus to help her. So many things had happened in the past week, all of them affecting each of her family members in different ways. What could she say to them to address all of their concerns? Turning to Jesus in her time of need seemed to be becoming a pattern for Amy. Still, in her heart, she knew Jesus didn't mind. Instinctively, she understood this was what she was supposed to do, and it was as He intended it to be.

Taking a deep breath and a leap of faith, she called her children to come and sit beside her. She believed they were old enough to know the truth, and she didn't know what information they had been given, or by whom at this point. It was time to discuss the events of the last week with them, answer any questions they might have, and attempt to put their minds at ease, if at all possible. Somehow, through Jesus, Amy knew it was possible.

First telling her children that she loved them very much, Amy took both of them by the hand and told them she wanted them to know the truth about what had happened to her. She told them, generally, what had happened and then asked them if they had any questions.

Justin wanted to know where the man was who had hurt his mother and if he would be back. Amy didn't have an answer to that one. She assured both of her children she was going to be fine and that they were safe because the police were watching the house, but mostly, because Jesus was watching over all of them.

The police had assured Amy and Tom that they were reasonably certain the man who attacked her would not return. However, precautions were being taken to insure the safety of the entire family. Amy confided she was hoping the police would find the man soon and put him in jail, but she did believe they were all safe.

She explained the bruises would fade and that her bones would heal, and in time, this whole incident would be nothing more than a distant memory. Wanting to believe these things herself, Amy was very convincing with her children, and they seemed to relax a little more.

Amy told Abby and Justin she thought she was going to die at one point during the ordeal. She said that she was headed to heaven moving toward this incredibly bright and calming light, when Jesus told her it was not her time to go. She explained Jesus said He had work for her to do and that she must go back.

"He gave me an angel to watch over me and keep me safe," Amy told her children. "'When I was most afraid, I know it was my angel who kept me alive and brought me through all of this," she continued. "I know Jesus wants me to do something here on earth, and now I must learn what that might be and do all He may ask me to do. He'll give me strength to face everything this life may bring. I wish I could put into words what an incredible feeling it was to be so close to Jesus. I felt so at peace right then. I'm looking forward to going back someday."

"When Jesus gave you this angel, why didn't the angel stop the man from hurting you? Why didn't the angel just bring you home to us and stop the man from hurting you, Mom? I don't understand," Justin questioned trying to understand something that was clearly not easy to comprehend.

"I'm not sure I know how to answer this, but I'll try," Amy answered in an effort to alleviate her son's confusion. "You see, all of us have our own free will, and we may use it as we choose. Obviously, the man who attacked me chose to do the things he did because he wanted to do them. Jesus kept me alive in spite of what this person did or wanted to do. Even if this man had killed my body, I know he could not have touched my soul. God has power over all things, and in the end, it is His will that must be done. The angel Jesus has given to me will help me now through whatever I must do. I truly believe this. One day, when my work here on earth is over, I'll go to heaven to be with Jesus. But, for now, I must follow my heart and try to follow where Jesus will lead me. Yes, this was truly an awful thing that happened to me, but I know Jesus will help me every step of the way. I hope someday to be able to help others in some way. Jesus will help me to claim a victory of faith, and in His name, good will triumph over evil. If we believe, it always will."

Justin asked, "What does your angel look like, Mom? Does she have wings and wear a long white robe, and have a halo like all of the pictures we see?"

"To tell you the truth, I honestly don't know. I haven't actually seen the angel, or at least I don't think I have. I've felt a presence around me from time to time, and I think what I'm feeling is the spirit of the angel. I'm not at all sure that we can see angels at all. An angel might just be a spirit. Maybe one day I'll be able to answer that question for you, but for now, I honestly don't know."

"Jesus did good, Mom," Abby said, as she hugged her mother. "I love you. I'm glad you weren't alone through all of this. Maybe I can help you, too, with whatever it is that Jesus wants you to do. If you need me, I'll be here for you. I love you, Mom," Abby offered as she wiped tears from her eyes.

Justin hugged his mother and told her that he loved her, too. The fear Amy saw in her son's eyes earlier was now replaced with tenderness and at least

77

some degree of understanding. He seemed to accept his mother's explanation and appeared to be genuinely relieved.

Reassuring her children one last time, Amy said, "I'll be fine now. I'm not afraid, and as ugly as this whole thing was, something good has already come out of it. I'm closer to God now, much closer than I ever been before, and I have an angel. This is a very good thing."

Amy's arm and ankle were in casts, and her shoulder was in a brace. She had a difficult time maneuvering in the wheel chair or on the crutches she was using. Even though Amy found this to be frustrating, she recognized this to be only a temporary situation. Mostly, she was grateful that Jesus had spared her life. Now she was looking at her life as a precious gift to be used in service to God and for a greater purpose. She felt blessed to be here at all. Amy had been touched by death and had survived through the grace of God, and she knew it.

With determination, Amy decided she was not going to be a victim. She was a survivor and was going to make her life really mean something. This man may have hurt her body, but he could not touch her soul. He was never going to have that satisfaction. In Jesus name, Amy would not give that much power to him. Jesus was the winner in this case and she was determined to show the world how powerful the love of God truly is. Whereas she may have a long road stretched out before her, she was never again going to have to walk alone.

Amy went to bed that night thinking Tom would be by her side. He wasn't. He came home late from work, came in and said good night, and then said he would stay in the spare bedroom so he wouldn't hurt her while moving around in bed. Amy really wanted him to stay with her, but didn't say anything when he insisted that staying in the other room was a better idea. Again, she felt the distance between them widening.

As the days turned into weeks, Tom was attentively and dutifully caring for his wife when he was home, which wasn't often, and when others were around. But if they were alone, things seemed awkward between them. It was as if he was fulfilling some kind of obligation and Amy was becoming acutely aware of his coolness toward her and his lack of compassion.

Tom never spent the night with Amy, opting always to sleep in the spare bedroom. He was also spending as much time as he could at work. Amy was crushed by his distant attitude but remained silent realizing he, too, had been through a lot. She was hoping as the injuries faded and the physical reminders of the attack disappeared, Tom's attitude toward her would improve. This was a very difficult time for Amy, because she needed her husband now more than ever, and he seemed to need her less and less every day.

Six weeks passed and Tom was still distant and avoiding any situation where he might be alone with Amy. Returning home from the clinic where her casts were removed, Amy made a special dinner and planned to spend some quality time alone with her husband that night. Abby and Justin were both going to spend the night with friends, and Tom and Amy would have the house to themselves for the first time since a while before the attack. Her bruises had faded and the casts and braces were finally gone, so any visual reminders of the attack had now vanished. Amy was hoping this time would help to rekindle the spark that was now missing in their relationship.

When Tom arrived home from work, late as usual, Amy had a lovely dinner ready, and she was waiting for him. They ate but had very little conversation. Amy wanted to feel close to Tom again and needed some reassurance from him that everything was going to be all right between the two of them. She wasn't getting that from Tom. Mostly, there were long awkward silences followed by more long awkward silences. The gentleness they once shared seemed to be missing, and Amy missed it horrifically. She wanted Tom to hold her. Nothing more, just hold her. Was that asking so much?

Susan, her friend and rape counselor, had told Amy to give Tom some space and not to force the issue, but it had been more than seven weeks now since the attack, and he was becoming increasingly distant with every passing day. Amy needed him more and more, and Tom seemed to be colder and less comfortable around her with every passing hour. She had to do something. Somehow, she knew it was time.

"Tom, did you notice the casts are gone? I saw Doctor Veil today and he said he thought my body has healed well," Amy said, hoping to open the conversation. "Would you like some coffee? Honey, I'd like to talk to you," Amy said, as she got up and moved toward the coffee pot.

"I'm tired. I had rough day, and I don't really want to talk," Tom stated abruptly, almost defensively.

Amy had noticed the gentleness had been gone from his voice for weeks now. The coldness between them intensified and she felt they were losing touch with one another. Amy wanted to talk. She needed to talk. She needed him and didn't want to force the issue, but she was frustrated with things the way they were. She wondered why he didn't miss her as much as she was missing him. She had even begun to wonder if Tom had stopped loving her completely.

She and Tom had not spoken about the attack since she was in the hospital. Thinking back about it, she wasn't even sure if they talked about it at all. He may have been present while she was questioned by the police a couple of times, but she didn't remember if they ever really talked about any of this. He was clearly avoiding the entire subject, and Amy was feeling more pressured and upset by the minute because of it.

They were always so close before, or at least Amy thought they were. Now she felt as if he were a thousand miles away, even though he was sitting less than four feet from her. This was really starting to hurt Amy, and she wanted to make things better. Something inside her forced her to try to speak that which was in her heart.

"Tom, please. We need to talk. I need to talk," Amy tried once again to reach out to her husband.

"How could you let this happen, Amy? Why didn't you check the back seat of the car before you got in? What the hell were you thinking? Damn it, don't you ever think before you do anything? It was that job you had to have," Tom yelled out at her trying to place the blame for the attack squarely on her.

Angrily he shouted, "Now you expect me to believe you can't remember anything about this animal you had sex with! I'm not so stupid as to believe that crap! Why don't you try to tell it to somebody who's ignorant enough to believe it! For God sake, Amy, how stupid do you think I am? I don't want to deal with any of this. I don't want to deal with you! You've ruined my life, your life, the kid's lives, and now I'm the guy who's expected to pick up all the pieces and fix it. Well, I can't fix it. I don't know how to, and I don't want to. I'll never forgive you for this, Amy! Never!"

Amy felt as if Tom had stabbed her through the heart. She was devastated and ran crying to the bedroom. Tom left the house in a fit of anger and rage slamming the door behind him. What could she say? Amy fell onto the bed sobbing and shaking uncontrollably. She felt as if she had been raped for a second time but this time by someone she loved and trusted.

As she lay alone in the dark retracing her every move of that horrible day more than seven weeks ago, Amy began to question everything that happened. Was it her fault? Could she have stopped it? Could she have avoided or foreseen it? Sobbing and alone there in the night, Amy felt real, overwhelming guilt about the attack for the first time. Was it really her fault? Had she ruined everyone's lives. As she lay there in the night, she felt sick and alone questioning, wondering, and hurting.

She didn't have sex with this man! How could he say that? How could he think it? This animal almost killed her. How could Tom accuse her of something like that? Surely, he knew her better than that, didn't he? Was she trying to hide from the truth herself? Was it all her fault? Everything was so confused in Amy's mind now.

Sick to her stomach, Amy went into the bathroom. Vomiting from the shear pressure of the situation, she sat on the floor by the toilet, sick and crying. This very real emotional pain had overwhelmed her, and she felt broken inside. All of the events of the past seven weeks hit her with an incredible impact she was not prepared to handle. Her heart ached with a pain unlike anything she had ever felt before. The injustice of this world fell on her as if to crush the very life from her. She found herself wondering if there was anything left to live for. She questioned whether she should try to go on or simply sit there and die.

Standing up, moving to the sink, and splashing water on her face, Amy looked into the mirror. There, before her stood a woman she no longer recognized. The bruises had faded and the casts were gone, but she realized for the first time her life would be forever changed.

Unsure of how she felt about this fact, Amy felt violated in a way she had never felt before. Hadn't she been through enough? Was she ever going to have her life back? Wasn't what happened to her bad enough in and of itself? Does she have to live with the outrage of her husband who was now feeling the need to punish her for what a rapist did? Amy felt anger toward her husband for the things he'd said and for his attitude. She also felt guilty because she was angry.

Was she so different now, or was it Tom who had changed completely? She couldn't believe this was the same man she married and had a life with for more than 18 years! Was this the same man who used to hold her in his arms and whisper to her how very much he loved, wanted, and needed her? Amy wondered where the man she loved had gone. Something felt so terribly wrong to her. She felt in conflict with her husband and she also felt conflict within herself.

Who Amy had been before the attack no longer mattered. Amy began to realize that where she would go from here would be what would count when it was all said and done. She had been determined not to let this attack destroy her life, and now it was feeling more and more as if it had. Amy hated that feeling and felt as if all of this could drag her down to a place she really didn't want to go.

Desperately needing a lifeline at that moment, Amy reached out to God in prayer. Recognizing her spirit was in need of help, Amy prayed, "My Father, in Jesus name, help me. Lord, lift my spirit and give me strength. Forgive my sins and help me to be a better person. Give me faith and help me through this night. Please, Lord, give me peace. In Jesus name, I give my life to you. Show me what you need me to do. Give me the strength to do it, and help me to follow. Amen."

Amy washed her face and took a deep breath. She did feel better now. She didn't know how things were going to work out, but in the end she knew they would. No matter what happened now, Amy knew Jesus was with her. Her spirit would forever be with Him in heaven someday. She found peace in that fact. If all else was gone, this was something no one could take from her. No one.

She reached for the phone wanting and needing to talk to a friend. Amy dialed Terri's number, but the answering machine picked up. Terri had come to the hospital once while Amy was there, and she hadn't talked with her since. During that short visit at the hospital, Terri said she had business out of town, but Amy hoped she would have been back by now. Apparently she wasn't. Wishing Terri had been there, Amy decided not to leave a message. Instead, she decided to try to call her again tomorrow.

In the nightstand beside her bed, Amy had placed a book which Susan had given to her. She had read part of it while in the hospital, but had put it in the drawer when she came home, and she didn't look at it again, until now. Feeling lost and alone, Amy picked the book up and began looking through it. Maybe something in there would help her to understand some of this or perhaps give her some comfort.

Curling up on her bed, she began to read through the table of contents when she saw a chapter titled *"Is There Life After Rape?"* In this chapter she read things about dealing with the aftermath of rape. It also addressed the issue of helping your significant other to do so, too. Hoping to find answers, Amy read the entire chapter. Reading about how many men react negatively to their wife being raped often blaming her for the attack, she recognized this behavior was maybe part of his healing process. Perhaps with time, he would see things differently. Amy prayed he would.

"I have to go on with my life. Tom may never be ready to accept me back into his life again. Maybe he will, and maybe he won't," Amy said to herself. She had to take care of herself now, and for the first time since the rape she realized and acknowledged that Tom would have to find his own way back to her and to their relationship if he chose to do so. This was honestly his choice to make, and she needed to trust Jesus to carry this burden for her. Conceding that these things were really out of her hands, Amy knew she must move forward.

She promised herself that she would do everything she could to find her attacker in an effort to stop him from doing this to anyone else. She would deal with each problem as it came and stop worrying about things she had no real control over. Accepting each day as it came made more sense to Amy now, because she finally realized she can't fix everything, nor should she try. She had to leave these burdens with Jesus. It was time for Amy to learn to follow her heart.

"Jesus, you gave me an angel. I thank you for that gift. Precious Lord, please help me. I've felt so lost and alone, and now I've found peace with you. Thank you. Please Lord, what do you want me to do? What is it you would ask of me? Show me, lead me, and I will follow. Teach me. Guide my steps. Help me to fix what you want me to fix and leave to you the things I should leave alone. I believe you will be with me every step of the way," Amy prayed, knowing Jesus was with her now.

Before Amy fell asleep that night, she picked up her Bible and clutched it tightly to her chest. When she fell asleep, along with sleep, came peace. In the morning, as Amy went to get out of bed, her Bible tumbled to the floor. It fell open and as she reached down to picked it up, the sunlight glistened through the window, and illuminated the page. She sat back on the bed and read the passage that had been lighted.

This passage was St. John 14 verse 26, and it reads as follows: "But the comforter, which is the Holy Ghost, whom the Father will send in my name, He shall teach you all things, and bring all things to your remembrance, whatsoever I have said unto you."

Amy started her day with a prayer, that in Jesus name, He would be with her and light her way. She asked for help to face whatever may come her way. She also prayed for peace in her soul and for added faith.

Dressing quickly, she ran down the hallway. Tom had not returned home. He had never stayed away before like this, and Amy knew something was really wrong. Should she call him at work? Maybe she should wait to see if he called her first? What should she say to Abby and Justin when they arrived home from their overnight visit with friends? Should she wait to hear from Tom or go out looking for him? No. She decided to simply wait to see what the day would bring.

At about 11:30 a.m., Justin came home. He didn't notice that his father wasn't there and didn't ask. When Abby came in, she asked Amy if she felt all right, and Amy said she was just fine. With no more questions being asked, Amy relaxed a little. At least if the kids didn't ask about Tom, she wouldn't have to say anything.

At about 2:15 p.m. the doorbell rang, and Amy ran to answer it. There stood a man she sort of remembered from when she was in the hospital. He was one of the detectives who worked her case. He asked if she had remembered anything else about the attack that might be of help to the authorities. Amy hadn't remembered anything else at all. The detective, Steven Dunne, had a request he wanted Amy to consider. He thought if she went under hypnosis, perhaps she would remember something that could help with the investigation.

This wasn't the first time this had been suggested, but before, her husband had objected and refused to allow Amy to do it. This time, Tom wasn't here by his own choice, and she felt free to follow her heart and do what she thought was right. Amy really wanted to see the rapist caught and prosecuted. If she could remember something to help the authorities find him, what could be the harm? She would have done this willingly weeks ago if Tom would have allowed it. Now, it just felt right to say yes, so she did.

Amy agreed to see the doctor who was going to hypnotize her on that next Monday at 9:00 a.m., and Mr. Dunne offered to pick her up and take her to this appointment. But Amy felt she could handle it on her own and thanked him for the offer. The insurance company had replaced her car, and she was able to drive again, so she didn't think she'd need a ride. She thought it was nice of him to ask, and she assured him she would be fine going on her own.

It was about 8:30 p.m. that evening when Tom finally called. Amy met his call with very mixed feelings. He said he thought it would be better if he stayed away for a few days stating he needed some time to think and a little space. He told Amy he really didn't want to hurt her, but he thought this would be best for everyone, under the circumstances. Fighting back tears, Amy hung up the phone. She had wanted a different response from Tom. Still in her heart she knew she had to accept his decision. In a way, she was a little relieved that she wouldn't have to put up with Tom's indifference toward her. She wasn't sure if she could handle much more of that. Maybe this was a blessing in disguise.

When Justin and Abby asked where their father was, Amy told them that he would be gone for a few days. Justin assumed it was business, because Tom's job often took him out of town. But Abby knew something was wrong. When Justin left the room, Abby asked Amy what was going on? Amy tried to explain as simply as she could without going into too much detail, but Abby kept pressing the issue. Indeed, Abby had noticed how distant Tom had been, too. Amy was beginning to realize how children are affected by the problems of their parents, and she made every effort to calm Abby's fears.

Finally Abby confessed to her mother; she had come back home that night when she went to stay with her friend. She said she overheard Tom accusing Amy of being at fault for the attack when she came in to get her jacket. Abby admitted she was angry with her dad, and she slipped back out of the house quietly so no one would know she had been there and heard anything. Abby thought her father was very unfair and exceptionally cruel.

Finally, Amy told her daughter the whole truth. She said, "Sometimes the husband of a rape victim has a lot to deal with, too. He just needs some time to think about things and get himself together. This isn't at all unusual, and we just have to be patient and give him time to work through all of this in his own way and in his own time. I think he feels powerless to do anything about the situation, and he wants this man to be caught and put in jail as much as I do. On some level, he probably feels the need to see someone punished, and maybe he even feels a little guilty because he wasn't able to stop the attack from happening in the first place. I think most husbands feel like they should take care of their wives and keep them safe. Even though there was nothing he could have done to prevent the attack, on some level, he probably thinks he should have. It doesn't have to make sense. If he's feeling these things, he's feeling them. Given some time, hopefully he'll feel better soon, and then we'll work on all of these issues together. We need to be patient."

Abby wasn't usually an outspoken person, but she was shocked and upset by her father's reaction and his anger, and she said to Amy, "Mom, how can he blame you for this? What's wrong with him, Mom. You deserve better than this. Don't you think he should be here with us now to protect all of us from this maniac? This is so lame, and I think Dad is completely wrong. If someone had raped me, would he walk away from me, too? There's something wrong with this, Mom. It's just not right! I should have said something that day when

I overheard him saying those awful things, but I didn't. Now, I wish I had. I don't like Dad very much, anymore. He's changed. Dad's never home anymore. Even before you were raped, he was always off working or running somewhere. He never has time for any of us anymore, and it's been that way for a long, long time. Where is he now? I want to talk to him."

"Abby, I don't know where he is. He didn't tell me. In any case, Honey, we have to be patient and give him some time. I wish I could make you feel better about this," Amy said as she tried to console her angry daughter, finally realizing it didn't help.

"Dad's being a Jerk. I hope he stays away forever," Abby said angrily as she ran up the stairs to her room. With the slamming door, Amy accepted that the conversation was over. At least for now.

When Abby emerged from her room later, she didn't mention their earlier conversation again, and Amy decided that spending some quality time with her daughter was more important than trying to explain Tom's actions, so nothing more was said at the time. Amy spent the rest of the weekend with Abby and Justin. They played games, watched movies, talked and took a couple of walks.

On Monday morning, Amy was just about ready to leave to see the doctor who was going to hypnotize her when the doorbell rang. Grabbing her purse and a sweater in an effort to save time, she went to answer the door on her way out. First looking through the glass to see who was there, Amy was relieved to see Mr. Dunne.

"I see your ready to go," said Mr. Dunne, who was standing outside the door. "I didn't feel right about asking you to do this on your own and thought the least I could do would be to offer you a ride. I hope you don't mind. Please, call me Steven."

"No, that's fine, Steven. Thank you," Amy said as she locked the door behind her. "I'm glad I don't have to go alone, and you may call me Amy. I guess I'm a little nervous about this," she admitted as she fumbled with her key while trying to lock the door as they left.

On the way to the doctor's office, Steven filled Amy in on the information they had gathered on her case. He told her an elderly woman who lived close to the store where she had been shopping just prior to the attack had seen a man who was sitting in an old gray station wagon. The man got out of the vehicle once and walked around it so she got a pretty good look at him. She had given them a good description of this man. He was about 5'10" tall, weighed about 180 pounds, had brown short hair cut in a crew cut, and wore sun glasses. He was unshaven, looked dirty, and was wearing a dark green jacket. He seemed out of place just sitting in his car just watching people. The woman had gotten a phone call and went into the kitchen to answer it. When she returned, the man was gone.

The description the woman gave of the man didn't jar any memories for Amy. She hoped the hypnosis would help. She wanted her assailant arrested and put into jail and told the detective that she was very uncomfortable with the fact that he was still at large. She feared not only for herself, but also for her family as well as anyone else he might eventually hurt.

Arriving at the clinic, Amy was more than a little nervous. This was to be expected under these circumstances, but knowing this didn't make it any easier for her. Steven said he had several appointments to keep, but another officer would be waiting to take her home when she was finished with the doctor.

After meeting Dr. Heinz, they talked for a while, and she was able to help Amy feel a little more relaxed. Understanding the procedure seemed to help. While under hypnosis, everything was being recorded on both video and audio tape. Amy agreed to this for two reasons. First, she wanted to see and hear the tapes for herself, hoping she might find answers to her many questions. Second, she wanted the police to have the best possible information in a more first hand way. Amy's primary goal here was to help the authorities apprehend the assailant before he could harm anyone else.

Amy listened to the audio tape after the session. While reviewing the tape recording with Dr. Heinz, Amy realized she had in fact seen the man's face clearly in the mirror before he began to strangle her. She described him in detail while under hypnosis.

The tape was very difficult for Amy to listen to. She broke down crying several times during the review of the fifty-two minute ordeal she revisited while under hypnosis. Amy remembered several things: She had seen the man briefly, but clearly, in the back seat of her car before he began to strangle her, and she was able to describe him in great detail. She remembered seeing the bright light, feeling its warmth, and hearing the voice of Jesus. Amy spoke about the angel she was given by the Lord, and she recalled that she wanted to stay in that place, but knew she had to return to her body and come back to finish the things Jesus would ask of her.

After that point more memories began to emerge as she listened to the tape. Amy remembered when she awoke from the initial strangulation, she was being beaten and kicked by her attacker because he wanted her to wake up. It seemed that he had taken great pleasure in watching his other victims suffer in the past, and he wanted her to know what was happening to her. He wanted her awake and aware of the horror he intended to put her through. She could remember the sound of his voice as he was telling her this. She also recalled hearing his laughter. He sounded sick and deranged. He mocked her cries for help as she lay crouched on the floor of the car trying to protect herself from further injury to her head as he beat her repeatedly with some kind of stick.

She remembered she was on the front passenger side of the car as he was driving her car. She felt the car swerve and sway when he would reach over to hit her again and again. Fearing for her life, Amy knew she had to do something. This man intended to rape and kill her, and he took a great deal of pleasure in telling her that this was in fact his plan. As Amy felt the car slowing slightly, she jumped from the moving vehicle, as she believed it to be her only real means of escape. When she did this, she didn't know where she was. She just knew she had to do it.

Amy remembered actually opening the car door, rolling out of the car, and feeling her body hit the gravel on the road. She must have lost consciousness at that point, although she had some faint memory of being kicked and hit while she was on the ground somewhere. Amy was unsure if this happened by the roadside where she had jumped out of the car, or if it was in the woods where he must have dragged her. The next thing she remembered was waking up in the woods a couple of times and finally crawling toward the highway where she was eventually found. Then she woke up in the hospital.

Physical evidence clearly proved she had been raped, but Amy had no real memory of that aspect of the attack. On at least some level, she thanked Jesus for that. Perhaps this was some of God's great mercy, her having no real memory of the rape itself. Maybe her angel wiped it from her memory, or perhaps she was unconscious at the time of the rape. This is something she may never know. In any case, she was glad she couldn't remember that part of this horror.

Now she had something to help the police to find her attacker. Amy did remember this man's face and she hoped to find him in a picture the police might have on file. Surely this was the same man the woman saw in the old gray station wagon. Amy's description of him would be the same, except that Amy could add the fact that his two top front teeth were broken off, he had gray-blue eyes and a scar on his left cheek that was about two inches long and shaped like a jagged, backward "C".

The officer that was waiting for Amy took her to the police station at Amy's request. Back at the police station, she looked through books of criminals for four hours, but found no one that looked like the man who had attacked her. Since she had to be home with her children soon, she was driven home by an officer but planned to return the next day to look through the photos again. Finding this man was now Amy's first priority. Remembering his face felt like both a blessing and a curse to her. Yes, she could identify him, but now the nightmare had a face. She shivered at the thought of having to see this man again.

When she returned home that day, Tom was there. This time he wanted to talk. Fearing his attitude of a few days ago, Amy reluctantly agreed. She'd had a rough day herself, but she also hoped Tom had managed to settle some of his own issues in his mind. She prayed he'd had a change of heart and wanted to be with her now. In any case, Amy was hopeful.

Tom told her he was sorry for the things he said and the way he left that night. He wasn't trying to add to the problems she was already facing, but he was unable to deal with the fact that his virgin bride had been with another man, regardless of the circumstances.

He recognized the fact the attack wasn't really her fault and that she shouldn't feel guilty about it, but he wasn't sure if he could ever get beyond it. He hoped she could understand his feelings about this. In any case, he wasn't ready to come home and was unsure if he would ever be. He wanted her to know he didn't really blame her for all of this, but he wasn't sure he could forgive her completely for making the "mistake" which made it possible for the attack to happen.

Amy stood in her own kitchen looking at the man she had been married to for 18 years, and wondered who he was? This man was like a stranger to her now. She didn't know what to say. She didn't know what she was supposed to feel. She only knew he was not the answer. The man with whom she shared everything and trusted with her life was now nothing more than an empty shell standing before her with no real feeling for her. He stood before her emotionless, lacking passion, void of compassion and commitment.

Quietly and simply, Amy asked Tom to leave. He said he'd call in a day or two, but she felt there was little more to be said. In the short space of eight week's time, her life had crumbled beneath her and had shaken her to her core. As Tom left that day, Amy realized he never mentioned anything about Abby or Justin. He didn't even ask how they were. Amy knew that Tom was honestly leaving all of them. He was just walking away as if they never meant anything to him at all.

When Abby and Justin came home, Amy was still in shock. She prepared dinner for them, cleaned the kitchen, and went to her room, stating she wasn't feeling well. No one questioned her and Amy was glad, because she wasn't in the position to answer any questions at the moment. She needed a little down time to reflect on everything that had happened that day.

Alone in her room later that night, Amy lay staring at the ceiling, wondering where her life had gone. All of the things her husband had said to her cut like a knife. She remembered the conversation with her daughter a few days before, and too, wondered if Abby had been the one who was raped, how her husband would have handled that? Would he have left her, too? What was she thinking? He was leaving Abby and Justin now because she had been raped. How could he just walk away? Didn't he care how much he was hurting his children?

Now she was left to tell the children what was going on. Tom hadn't seen them in five days now, and he never even asked about them. Amy never imagined Tom could spend this much time away from Abby and Justin and not even bother to ask how they are or even if they needed anything. She was beginning to question whether she ever really knew Tom at all.

At breakfast the next morning, Amy realized that Abby and Justin were leaving for summer camp for the next three weeks at 2:00 that afternoon.

Although she knew they were going to go, with all that had happened recently, it had slipped her mind. The kids had gone to this camp for the last two years, and they loved it. Amy knew she had to help to pull everything together in a hurry, but she believed this would be a good break for them and hopefully buffer them from all of the fallout of the past few weeks. Amy thought because Abby and Justin had been through a lot lately, camp would do them good. She hoped while they were gone, things might straighten out at home.

Busily Amy got Abby and Justin ready for the trip to camp. By 2:00 when their ride arrived, they were ready to go. She kissed her children goodbye and told them that she loved them. When Justin asked where his father was, Amy said he had gotten tied up at work and was unable to get home to see them off. She knew this was a lie, and she really didn't want to lie to him, but she thought this was not the time to go into all of that. Anyway, Tom's lack of interest in the children would only cause them pain should they find out about it. How could she tell them what was going on and then send them off to camp, expecting them to have fun? No, this was the better way of handling this situation.

Abby seemed reluctant to leave her mother alone apparently sensing there was more than Amy was saying. But with a reassuring smile and a hug from her mother, Amy finally convinced Abby she would be fine and that she really needed some time alone. Camp would be good for all of them. Promising to call, the children finally were on their way.

Waving goodbye to Abby and Justin as the van pulled away from the house, Amy felt a little empty inside. She knew Abby was aware of the problems between Tom and herself, and she was wishing her daughter didn't have to carry that knowledge with her. It all seemed so unfair. The children were too young to have to deal with the events of the last two months, but clearly it was inevitable at this point.

"Jesus, please keep my children safe and happy on this trip," Amy whispered as she walked back into the house. "Help me to find a way to make them understand all of this without causing them too much pain. Lord, help me to find a picture of the rapist. I'd feel better if he were locked up and couldn't hurt anyone else," continuing her little conversation with Jesus. As she reached for her purse and headed out to the police station, she asked, "Please help me fight my fears, Lord. Forgive my lie to my son. I really don't want to hurt him. I'll try to do better." With that, Amy drove off in her car.

When she arrived at the police station, she went over to the lady who had given her the books with the pictures of known offenders yesterday and was given a few more books to look through. For the next four hours Amy looked at pictures hoping to find the man who raped her. Opening the last book, which had been placed on the desk next to her, she heard a familiar voice and turned to see Steven who had just entered the police office.

89

"Well hello, Amy. I didn't know you were coming in today," Steven said with a smile. "This is a pleasant surprise. Did you find anyone?"

"Unfortunately, no," Amy stated, clearly disappointed as she went back to looking through the pictures.

A few minutes later Steven came over and sat across from Amy and handed her a cup of coffee. She thanked him for it and then asked if there were any new leads in her case. Steven stated there weren't. When Amy finished looking through the book in front of her it was almost 6:45 p.m. and Steven pointed out that her children would be wondering where she was.

Amy explained that she had just sent both Abby and Justin off to camp for three weeks and that Tom wasn't home either. Realizing no one was waiting for her at home, Steven suggested that perhaps he should follow her back to the house to make sure she got there safely. But Amy said she would probably stop for dinner first, so it wouldn't be necessary. Steven hadn't eaten either and invited Amy to grab a bite to eat with him along the way and then he could still check the house before he went home. Not looking forward to going home to that big, empty house alone, Amy agreed to have dinner with Steven. If she were to be honest with herself, she'd have to admit the idea of going home alone was a little scary, and she wasn't looking forward to it.

Sitting at the local diner, Amy and Steven talked about the case at first, and then he asked if Tom was working late or away on business. Unsure of how to answer, Amy took a deep breath and told Steven the truth. Steven was very kind and understanding about her circumstance, and stated he had encountered that reaction from many husbands who have found themselves in similar situations. Some of them came around and dealt with the problems and stood by their wives, but many of them unfortunately didn't. He commented that he thought most of those men lived life with a double standard, one for themselves and another for the rest of the world. Steven didn't want to seem cynical, but cynicism often goes along with the territory referring to his career in law enforcement.

Steven explained that he never could understand how some men could have their house or business robbed or their car stolen and be able to see themselves as victims so clearly. But if his wife was raped, it somehow becomes her fault. When something is done against them, it's not their fault. But on the other hand, if their wife's dignity, honor, and sense of self worth had been stolen, compromised, or violated, she was somehow to blame and in some way is now less than she once was. Steven stated he often saw this reaction, but he said he had a hard time dealing with it and thought it was cruel and ironic how narrow minded some people can be.

Steven offered to talk to Tom to see if he could help him understand or see if there was anything he could do, but Amy asked him not to get involved. She really needed Tom to work this out on his own, and if he couldn't, she needed to know that, too. Steven seemed to understand.

As he and Amy talked, she found out that Steven had been married to a wonderful lady for sixteen years before she passed away from cancer almost four years ago. His job was now pretty much his life. They had no children, although they always wanted to, but it just never happened. He said he and his wife had talked about adoption, but when his wife was diagnosed with cancer, they started a seven year long battle that took most of their time and energy. In the end, the cancer ultimately took her life.

It was obvious to Amy that Steven loved and missed his wife very much. She found out his wife's name was Lisa. Amy noticed when he spoke about her, he did so with so much love and tenderness in his voice Amy could see this man had a great capacity for love and compassion. She saw gentleness in his eyes and sensed tenderness in his soul hidden beneath a gruff exterior.

Steven confided to her he had seen so much horror in this life while on the job as a police officer and now as a detective, that he had a very difficult time seeing the good in anything anymore. Before he lost his wife to cancer, she kept him grounded somehow. But since she's been gone, he felt as if he had little to hold on to, and chose to dive head first into his job hoping to make a difference in the lives of others.

While explaining he knew he shouldn't lose his faith in God, he said he'd found it difficult to see beyond all of the loss and pain he has seen and lived through in his own life. He also confided to Amy that when Lisa died, he felt as if the best part of him died, too. Now he wondered if he'd ever find love again, or if he would have to be alone for the rest of his life. Steven also stated he often struggled with himself to get up in the morning to face the day. Not many days were worth looking forward to anymore for him.

The sweet old waitress who had been serving them was cleaning the table next to theirs and apparently overheard Steven making that statement. She walked over to Amy's side and smiled at both of them, and with a wink told Steven and Amy, "Sometimes when we think we have lost everything, and even our faith seems gone, what we have really lost is hope. Often we have to open our hearts before we can open our minds to the things God wants us to feel in our souls. He doesn't take from us without giving us something in return. Perhaps, God has given each of you a gift you have not yet learned to recognize. Maybe, Jesus is asking something of you and you're not listening with your heart. We need to remember that love is after all, God's greatest gift. Have faith. Believe these things."

With that, she cleared the plates from the table and disappeared into the kitchen. This old woman seemed familiar to Amy, but she couldn't quite place where she may have seen her, or when for that matter. In any case, she seemed very sweet and thoughtful. Both Amy and Steven thought what she said made sense to them, and they did appreciate her input.

Before either Amy or Steven realized it, time had passed so quickly and it was about 10:00 p.m. Steven paid the bill, and they left the diner. Steven followed Amy home and then came in briefly to make sure no one was in the house and that Amy was safe. When he left, Amy thanked him for dinner and for checking the house and locked the door behind him. After she saw his car driving away, she went in to bed.

Getting out of the shower the next morning, Amy heard the phone ring and stepped into the hall to answer it. Susan, the rape counselor she talked to in the hospital, was calling to check on her. They hadn't talked for a few days and Susan was wondering how Amy had been getting along. They had a lot of catching up to do. Amy suggested they meet for lunch as she planned on stopping by the police station to finish looking through the photos they had on file.

She thought seeing Susan might help her sort through all of the things going on in her life. But more than this, she had started a friendship with this woman who had helped her so very much while she was in the hospital. Susan was a kind, intelligent woman who seemed to have a great deal of inner strength. Amy knew she had a family of her own and that she was married. However, she was aware that Susan had been living as a single mother for a while now, because of some marital problems. Aside from that Amy knew little else about her. She was hoping to get to know Susan a little better now as a friend.

At lunch the two women talked about the case at first but then shifted their focus to their personal lives. Amy explained that Tom had left her and he hadn't even asked to see the children. She couldn't understand how he could feel the way he did or behave the way he was behaving. It was as if the last 18 years of marriage had meant nothing to him, and his children had become people he no longer cared about. Something was so very wrong here, and Amy couldn't quite get a grip on the situation. Nothing seemed to fit anymore and it felt as if there were pieces of the puzzle missing.

Amy was troubled by this entire situation. With frustration beginning to set in, she was starting to feel more than a little angry with her husband. Both, because of his behavior, and because of his reaction to the situation, something about this didn't make any sense to her. And now, Amy had begun to wonder if things were as good between Tom and her as she once thought they were. Were things really okay between them before the attack? She wondered if there were signs of trouble she may have missed or possibly ignored through the years. Ever since Abby mentioned how often Tom was away from home and how little time he spent with his family, Amy had been thinking about the many nights he was working late or went out of town. She began to wonder where Tom might have been when he was supposed to be at the golf course or gym. She had always trusted him and never thought to question it until now, but she was developing some serious doubts about his honesty. She hated feeling this way and thinking these things, but still she wondered.

As the two women talked, Susan began to open up about her life, too. She told Amy, she had been married twice. Her first husband was an abusive alcoholic, and her second was going through what most people refer to as a mid life crisis. She was hoping he'd outgrow his current behavioral manifestation, but only time would tell. At the moment, she was living the life of a single parent but hoping for a reconciliation soon. In any case, she was determined to ride it out. Susan believed marriage should be a lifetime commitment if at all possible, and she wanted to save her marriage.

However, Susan knew sometimes these things are out of our hands. She told Amy that she prayed a lot. Amy was amazed at how together this lady was in spite of all of the things she had been through herself. She seemed to have so much grace under pressure and an incredible amount of compassion for others. The two women visited for quite a long time that afternoon. They both realized this was going to be a special and lasting friendship.

Amy went back over to the police station after lunch. When she arrived there, she spoke briefly with the officer who is in charge of such things and was given another set of books filled with pictures. As Amy turned from page to page, she began to feel as if this whole process was hopeless. After viewing countless photos, she had nothing to show for her efforts. Feeling frustrated with the whole idea of finding a picture of her attacker in one of those books, Amy took a deep breath and closed her eyes to rest them, and also to pray. She needed added faith just then and was feeling a little overwhelmed. It felt as if the past few months were closing in on her, and she needed a little extra comfort.

It was at that time she overheard two officers talking about another rape case. They mentioned Amy's name as they talked about some similarities between the two cases. This immediately got Amy's attention and she felt the need to go over to them and ask about the other case they mentioned. Both officers tried to side step Amy's questions, but finally realized she wasn't about to give up and go away. So they asked her to wait in the next room until someone could come in and talk with her privately.

As Amy sat in that room alone, many things ran through her head. She wondered why Steven hadn't told her about another rape, or if that was why he insisted on checking her house the night before. Was the other victim dead or alive, and where was she found? Is this maniac going to come after her again? Is she safe at home alone? Amy was really glad that Abby and Justin were gone now. At least she wouldn't have to worry about their safety.

When someone finally opened the door to the room she was waiting in, Amy was surprised to see Steven. He came walking in with two other men, and they all sat down around the table to talk. She was told, yes, another woman had been raped in a town seven miles away, and she was alive. The description of her attacker was similar to the description Amy gave of the man who attacked her. No, they had not made an arrest or found the man. This

93

attack happened at about 11:00 p.m. the night before and they planned to run tests to determine if this was, in fact, the same man who attacked Amy. However, she was told this would take time, and they would have to wait for results. They told Amy they did have a couple of leads, but nothing definite at the moment.

Of course Amy was very shaken by this. Seven miles isn't far away, so the rapist was still in the area. All of the officers suggested Amy should go to stay with friends or relatives for a couple of days, and she gladly agreed. It was decided she would stay with her sister Ann and her husband who lived about two miles from Amy's house.

After calling her sister to fill her in on the latest information and to tell her she was going to have a house guest for a few days, Amy left the police station and headed over to Ann's house. As she turned into Ann's driveway, Steven's vehicle pulled in right behind her. This surprised Amy, but she was also a little glad to see him.

It seems he wanted to know exactly where she was staying in case they needed her, and also he wanted to reassure her that it was unlikely this man would bother her again. But, he also stated caution is always advised and wise in these situations.

As they stood out in her sister's driveway talking, Amy began to see again just how caring and compassionate Steven really was. He genuinely cared about people, and in spite of the fact that he implied he had been hardened to life by his job, there was something there which was unmistakably kind and gentle about him. When she jokingly asked him if all of the cases he handled were given so much personal attention, his reaction surprised Amy a little.

Steven told her, "When your job is all you have left in your life, your cases become everything to you. Maybe it gets too personal sometimes, but I'm not sure I know how to change it. I'm not sure I'd want to, especially if you're part of that equation."

This took Amy by complete surprise, and she wasn't sure how to react to his statement. Luckily, she didn't have to, as his radio went off and he had to leave immediately. When she went into the house, her sister asked who the handsome gentleman was, and Amy explained he was investigating her case, and she told her sister what he had said.

Amy and Ann were close and always told one another everything as sisters often do. Ann knew all about Tom's reaction to the rape and his decision to leave his family. She was really quite angry with Tom and was very vocal about it, but Amy didn't want her problems with Tom to be an issue with all their friends and family. On the other hand, she didn't want to defend him either, and quite honestly, Amy felt as if she were in a "no win" situation.

Later that day, Tom called Amy and asked if they could meet somewhere to talk. He said he had been trying to call her for hours and finally thought Ann might know where she was. Agreeing on the time and place, Amy went to see Tom. Unsure of what to expect, she hoped for the best, but feared the worst. However, she was totally unprepared for what she had to deal with when she came face to face with Tom and discovered the worst she had feared was only the tip of the iceberg.

When she arrived at the designated place for their meeting, Tom was already there, obviously very nervous. Amy knew by the look on his face, this wasn't good. She asked him what was wrong. He tried to make small talk at first, but Amy didn't want to talk about the weather or anything else he might use to avoid saying what he had come to say to her. She knew him well enough to know there was something terribly wrong here, and she wanted to know what it was, now.

Reluctantly, Tom looked into her eyes, and after taking a deep breath, told Amy what he was trying so hard not to say. He explained he had been seeing someone else for almost three years now, and he wanted to marry the other woman. She was five months pregnant and he felt this was something he had to do. He believed it was the right thing to do, and he didn't want to continue to live the lie he had been living for so long now. He told her he still loved her very much, but he also said that he loved the other woman.

Amy was speechless. She felt numb and sick all at the same time. How could he have been involved with someone else for almost three years without her even having the slightest suspicion anything was going on? How was this possible? What did she miss? How could he have covered his tracks so well? Was the man she loved and trusted such a consummate liar that he could fool her for three long years never slipping up or making a mistake while using one lie to cover another?

As Tom continued to tell Amy the whole truth, she was even more shocked than she had been in the beginning when Tom confessed he was involved with Amy's oldest and dearest friend, Terri.

The two people she had trusted most in her life had betrayed Amy. How could either of them have done this? How could she have been so blind? There was nothing she could say. Fighting back tears and words she was about to choke on, Amy trembled. She could barely breathe. Unable to listen to another word, Amy got up and ran to her car. She wanted to lay down and die right then and there! The flood gates opened as a river of tears poured from her eyes. Automatically, she started her car and drove off into the night. Giving no thought to where or even what direction she was going, Amy just drove.

As tears blinded her, the ache in her heart made her slump in the seat from the shear pain of it. She had never experienced pain like this before in her life. Not even the rapist hurt her as badly as she hurt at this moment. Sickened at the thought of her husband's confession, Amy drove off recklessly into the night.

"Oh, My God! Why did you spare my life? Why couldn't I have just died that day? I had to live for this? Oh, God, no," Amy screamed out in pain uncontrollably. "Jesus, let me die, oh please! I don't want to live through this," she sobbed, choking on the thought of her husband in bed with her best friend. All the lies they both must have told her. What a fool she had been! At that moment in time, Amy truly wanted to die. Nothing anyone could have said to her at that point could have helped her. She felt as if this betrayal was sucking the life out of her soul. Was it possible to live after learning these truths? Amy wasn't sure. She didn't know if she even wanted to try. Completely unaware of time or space, Amy drove off into the night as if searching for a hole to fall into.

Suddenly, she saw a shadow of a form on the road in front of her car. Instinctively she swerved out to avoid hitting the unknown figure. As she maneuvered around the shadowy image before her, her wheel hit the gravel on the side of the road, and she lost all control of the car. Sliding sideways at first and then around in a circle, Amy's car came to rest at the bottom of a deep ditch and rested in some bushes.

Unable to get her car door open, Amy frantically tried to get the window down frightened that she may have hit someone with her car.

"Jesus, please let him be okay. Please, don't let me have hurt someone..." she prayed and begged Jesus for help, for the first time realizing how reckless her behavior had been. Pushing on the door, finally forcing it open, Amy sprang from the car and ran up the embankment, praying she had not killed someone.

There, on the ground half sitting and half lying, was the dark figure she had seen in her headlights. Still praying under her breath, Amy bent down to see if this person was dead or alive. As she knelt down to help the person, a feeble hand reached up gently touching Amy's face.

In a soft whispery voice, the old woman asked, "Are you all right, my Dear? That was a close one."

"I'm so sorry. I thought I killed you," Amy stated, as she held tightly to the woman who was still sitting on the ground. "Are you okay? Is anything broken? I'll get help. I have a mobile phone in my car. I'll run down to get it," Amy said, jumping to her feet as she started to move toward the ditch. "I'll be right back."

Amy ran down the hill and went into her car searching for her phone. Finding it, she tried to call for help, but it didn't work. She ran back up the hill to help the old woman. Sitting on the ground next to the woman, she explained she tried to call for help, but the phone wasn't working. Frantically, she had tried over and over again, but still, she couldn't get a dial tone.

"I'm fine, Dear. We'll just have to walk for help to get your car out," the old woman suggested. "Here, help me up."

"No, you shouldn't move. You may have broken something and moving could make things worse," Amy warned, trying to keep the old woman seated on the ground.

"Nonsense. I jumped out of your way; your car didn't hit me. Anyway, these old bones have seen much worse than this over the years. Just help me up, and I'll be just fine," pleaded the old woman.

Against Amy's better judgement, she helped the old woman to her feet. "I'm so sorry. I could have killed you. I can't believe I did that," confided Amy to the old woman as they stood there together in the night in almost total darkness.

"Now, now, I'm fine. Judging from the state you're in, I'm probably in better shape than you are. What's wrong Dear? Can I help you? Tell me what's wrong," the old woman urged Amy to open up. "Sit with me for a while on this log, and we can wait for someone to come. It's a long way back to town." Positioning herself on the fallen tree by the side of the road, the old woman made a sigh of relief and said, "There, that's much better."

After being reassured several times by the old woman that she was just fine, Amy sat next to her, and they began to talk. Now Amy wasn't one to open up to a stranger, but somehow this old woman seemed so sweet and caring Amy couldn't help but to pour her heart out to someone who obviously wanted to help. In any case, Amy soon told the whole story to this old woman, from start to finish, including all the ugly details. From the attack and rape to her husband's confession about himself and Amy's best friend, she opened up completely to the old woman. It wasn't a pretty picture, but Amy seemed to have a need to paint it. Amy poured out her heart, leaving nothing unsaid or left to the imagination.

When she had finished telling her story, the old woman reached over and gently touched Amy's hand, and with a smile said, "All of these things will pass, child. You were not alone as you faced each of these trials in your life, and you are not alone now. You have a giving and compassionate soul, and it will serve you well in this world and on into heaven. Far beyond this life, God knows all things. If He calls you and you chose to follow Him, it is His Spirit which will guide you. Jesus loves you. Your soul is one of His treasures. Surely you know His touch, truly you've felt His love and His strength and His presence. You have seen His miracles and felt His compassion surround you. Child, you have witnessed His Glory."

Knowingly and with love there in the darkness of night, the old woman continued to speak to Amy with love and compassion. She continued comforting Amy as she said, "When Jesus touched you at the gate of heaven, surely you felt His love and compassion. He felt every blow to your body when you were attacked. He was there with you through everything. Again, as you lay on the cold forest ground, truly it was He who encompassed your soul in His loving warmth and grace keeping you safe through the night. When you called out to Him, truly He answered. If not for Him, you would not be here now. You must trust Him. You must follow Him now."

"What is it He is asking me to do?" How am I to know I am doing His will and not mine? Please, tell me," begged Amy as she searched within her own soul for answers.

"If Jesus were here, how would He handle this, my Dear? Ask yourself this question," suggested the old woman. "You see, Amy," the old woman explained, "Jesus is here. He lives in the Spirit within your soul. He sees all things and knows all secrets. There is nothing we can hide from Him. As to what He would have you do, Jesus would have you forgive others, as He has forgiven you, my child. Totally, completely, and without reservation, this is how we must forgive. He forgave those who hurt and betrayed Him. He did this with love and compassion. He did this wholly and without anger needing no vengeance or retribution. When you cry out to Him, He, also, forgives you. When He has forgiven you, what you did is gone. You are made clean again and you become pure in His eyes. You must learn to forgive others in this same way, Amy."

"The rapist, my husband, my friend? How?" Amy began to question, almost shocked at the thought of it.

"The rapist is a man consumed by Satan. Pray for the man, that his soul may be freed from the grip of the evil one. Pray that he will find his way out of darkness and into God's all consuming, forgiving light and grace. Do not condone the work of the evil one, but pray for those souls lost in his darkness that one day they might be free," offered the old woman.

As she continued to speak, the clouds drifted away from in front of the moon, and the light shown on Amy's face as the tears rolled down her cheeks. Hearing these things touched Amy's heart in a way it had never before been touched.

Amy listened intently as the old woman continued to speak. "You have chosen a partner in life who has betrayed your trust. The choices he has made are unworthy of both of you. Pray for him, too, Amy," suggested the old woman, "that he might see the error of his ways. Then, you must forgive him, and letting him go, allow him to find his own way. It is not your place to judge or punish him. You must allow him to seek his own path, as each of us must, just as you will need to seek yours. Conflicting spirits cannot abide together in harmony. You were in danger long before you were attacked. Your marriage was in trouble many years ago, because you were unequally yoked with a man who is not whom he pretends to be. It is for you to decide which path you will take through this life. Your husband must decide which path he will take."

"Remember it is not your place to judge or punish your friend, or your husband," said the old woman. "Pray for them, forgive them, and go forward, doing all Jesus may ask of you. Trust Jesus, Amy. It is He who will comfort you and give you peace. Anger is not of God. Evil is not of God. You, my child, must accept those things which you can not change and go on. You have the strength to do this, and you are not alone. Jesus loves you. Walk with Him, Amy. Walk with Him."

As tears of joy and compassion replaced those of anger and despair, Amy felt peace within her soul. This was a peace she had never before experienced, a peace even greater than that which she felt when she surrendered her life to Jesus while on her way to heaven during the attack. She knew the old woman spoke the truth. Amy prayed she would have the strength and the faith to do what she now knew was right.

Looking into the face of the old woman, as the moon cast its light down upon them, Amy recognized the old woman sitting by her side. She had brought her nourishment in the hospital when Amy needed hope. She had served Steven and her in the diner when they had dinner, speaking to both of them, telling both of them they needed to have faith. Now, she sat beside her in the night on a log teaching her about forgiveness, charity, compassion, and love.

"You're my angel," Amy stated, suddenly both feeling and understanding this was true beyond question. Knowing it from within the depths of her soul, Amy felt comfort and love far beyond anything the human tongue can tell.

"It was you who showed me there was hope and then led me to believe that I must have faith. Now you're teaching me about charity and forgiveness," Amy said as she touched the face of the old woman. With so many questions racing though her mind, Amy blurted out, "How will I know what I should do? How will I know which path I should take? Will you be with me always? What if I make a wrong choice or decision? How will I..."

With eyes filled with love, the old woman simply smiled and said, "When you were a small child and you chose to befriend the little boy with the funny clothes when the other children were teasing and taunting him, you made the choice to follow Jesus. As you grew older, when you told your friend you wouldn't take the candy from the store because you knew it was wrong, you made the choice to follow Jesus. When you volunteered to help at the hospital and spent time holding the old man's hand because he feared the unknown, and you sang *Jesus Loves Me* to him, again you chose to follow Jesus. All of these things you did out of love and compassion because you wanted to help someone. You chose to do the things Jesus would have you do. He has always been with you Amy, because you wanted Him to be with you. He is with you now."

For the first time, Amy knew she could do all Jesus would ask of her. Yes, she had been through a lot, but now she knew she was not alone. Her heart was full and her soul had been lifted. Amy recognized the fact that she now had so very much she could give to others.

Amy knew what she must do, and she believed she would have the strength to do it. Jesus was with her, and she understood she no longer had to walk through this life alone. She recognized the fact that she honestly had never really been alone, for Jesus had always been with her. Even as a small child, He had been there.

The emptiness and betrayal that had overwhelmed her over the past two months had now been replaced with a sense of peace, faith and hope. All the tragedy in her life now seemed to pale in the light of God's greater plan and glory, and Amy felt complete somehow as she sat on the log beside the old woman.

From a distance, they saw lights moving toward them. This was the first vehicle they had seen since Amy's car went into the ditch more than three hours before. Amy stood up and went closer to the road to flag down the vehicle hoping it would be someone who could summon help.

The vehicle coming down the road turned out to be an old tow truck. The man pulled Amy's car out of the ditch and looked it over. Nothing had been damaged and Amy was going to be able to drive home. She had traveled about sixty miles from home before going into the ditch, and she knew it would take an hour or more to get back. She paid the tow truck driver and offered to drive the old woman home, but the old woman declined saying she lived up the other direction, and the nice gentleman in the tow truck would drop her off. Amy really wanted to drive home with the old woman. She wanted to spend more time with her. But when she insisted it was better that she go in the tow truck, Amy knew it was time to say goodbye to her angel.

Amy reached out to hold the old woman and they embraced. Not wanting to let her go, Amy held on tightly and whispered, "Thank you. You saved my life. I don't want you to go. Will I see you again? You've given me a gift I will never forget. How can I ever repay you?"

Gently, the old woman kissed Amy's cheek and said, "Walk with Jesus, my child." With that she got into the tow truck with the driver and they drove off into the night.

Amy climbed into her car and headed for home. Home. Would it ever be the same? She didn't know what the future would hold, but she knew whatever happened from now on, she was going to be just fine. Armed with the knowledge that Jesus was with her, now and always, she was ready to face all life held for her.

As she drove toward home that night, she began to remember all the times she and the children went places and did things alone, because Tom was too busy. The more she thought about it, the more she realized how little time they had spent together as a family in the past few years. She remembered thinking how distant Tom had been with all of them. She wondered why she hadn't noticed it before? Amy was glad she could see things more clearly now.

Jesus was now a very real part of her life and nothing was ever going to change that. As she drove, Amy thoughtfully reflected on all of the events of the past few months. She felt at peace with herself and with her situation. As strange as this may seem, she felt truly relieved. The anger and rage she felt only hours earlier had now become little more than a distant memory.

When Amy arrived back at her sister's house, Tom's car was in the driveway. He had been sitting in the car waiting for her for hours now. He was visibly upset and extremely worried about her. It was obvious to Amy that Tom had very deep and conflicting feelings about everything that had happened in both of their lives recently. No longer feeling the sting Tom's words had inflicted on her earlier that evening, Amy knew it was time to let him go.

Hoping he would find his way through all of this and back to his children somehow, Amy walked over to him and gently said, "Tom, I'm sorry you've felt so conflicted and tied to me when what you really wanted was to let me go. I wish you'd have told me what you were feeling long ago. What's done is done, and neither of us can change it now. I guess I was caught up in raising the kids and managed to miss all of the signs pointing to the problems looming over my head. I'm sorry I didn't give you what you needed. I'm not sure either of us gave the other what we needed. All I know is that I'm not the same person I used to be and I feel very differently about what's important in my life now. I believe in God and in Jesus. I've seen heaven and have tried to tell you about these things, but you can't see it. I pray someday you will. I only know you and I aren't right together. I'm letting you go to find whatever it is you think you need. I hope you'll remain a part of our children's lives, but this too, will be another choice you'll have to make."

"I'm not sure what I want, Amy," Tom tried to explain, obviously thrown by the fact that Amy was willing to let him go so easily. "Maybe if we just took a little more time, I could figure out exactly what it is that I do want," he suggested.

"No, you have Terri in your life now, and she and your baby need you. As much as it hurt me to accept it, I know we don't belong together anymore. I forgive you, Tom," Amy said speaking gently and calmly to the man she had once committed her life to. "If we had belonged together, you'd never have been with Terri, or anyone else for that matter. I'm not angry. I was hurt by this more than anything, but I know it's time for us to move on," Amy stated calmly, trying to show Tom that she truly wanted him to be happy. "I have to do what I know is right in my heart, and I believe ending our relationship as we once knew it is right. I accept your choice to be with Terri. I'll have someone call you about the legal business. I hope you'll spend as much time as you can with the kids. I'm sure this will be difficult in the beginning for them and probably for all of us, but I know it's the right thing for us to do," Amy explained, reaching out to touch Tom's hand in an effort to comfort him. "I hope you find what you're looking for. I know I've found something that had been missing in my life until now. Go, be happy," Amy whispered as she walked away from Tom...

Amy didn't know the events of that April morning two months earlier would forever change her life, but they did. On that day as Amy dropped her children off for school and went to the grocery store, she didn't see the danger lurking over her shoulder, but it was. She was unaware that her marriage of 18 years had been crumbling beneath her, but it had. She didn't know that she'd find something she need her whole life, but she did. Despite the pain and horror of that day, as a result of it Amy found truth, hope, and inner peace. She was given a gift she will always treasure. She found Jesus.

Amy gave Tom the divorce, and he married Terri shortly thereafter. They had a beautiful little girl named Sarah. Unfortunately Tom and Terri's marriage ended in divorce within two years. Tom also had two more failed marriages after that, and he continues to struggle with the decisions he has made in his life. Tom also confessed to Amy that he had numerous affairs throughout their marriage. He often calls Amy expressing regret about the choices he's made along the way, wishing things were different between them. Amy still prays one day he will find peace in his life.

Amy and Terry have resumed their friendship after a couple of years and remain close today. Amy and her family often helped Terri while she was raising Sarah alone. Terri has learned what being a friend really means and she too, has found peace with Jesus. Terri has never remarried and lives alone with Sarah. She is thankful for her friendship with Amy.

Abby married and had two children. She is happy and remains very close to Amy and Justin. Abby's bond with her father has frayed over the years and is hanging only by a very thin thread. Tom sees Abby and her family only on the occasional holiday. Abby often says he feels more like a stranger than her father.

Justin is teaching and coaching in a small high school in the Midwest. He has recently married and is looking forward to having children. He volunteers to work with children who don't have fathers at a center in a nearby city. He tries to stay in contact with Tom, but they see one another only on those few occasional holidays. Justin had missed the years he lost with his father and promises to be a better parent when he has children of his own. Amy knows he will.

Susan reconciled with her husband and continues to be Amy's best friend today. She offered Amy a job at the crisis center when Amy was going through her divorce, and the two women are still working together at the center.

As for the rapist, he was never found. Amy has put him and all of the bad things about him and that time in her life behind her and has gone on with a full and productive life. She still prays her assailant will not hurt anyone else, but she no longer lives in fear. If her assailant ever raped again, Amy has no knowledge of it. Having turned her life over to Jesus, she has found peace.

As for Amy, she's still working at the crisis center helping others. About two years after Amy was divorced, she met a man who came to volunteer at the center after he retired from law enforcement. Yes, you guessed it; that would be Steven Dunne. Eight months later they were married and have been together ever since.

Amy and Steven have a wonderful marriage; they both believe in the things of God and are committed to helping others. Steven is now the father Abby, Justin, and Sarah need, and he loves all of them as if they were his own. Both he and Amy enjoy being grandparents and are looking forward to having more grandchildren in the future.

As for her angel, one day when Amy and Steven were helping to move Amy's mother into a senior building, they found an old family picture album in the attic of her mother's home. When they looked inside they saw a picture of Amy's angel. The angel was Amy's Great, Great Grandmother, Catherine. Both Amy and Steven recognized her immediately. Amy had never seen it before or even knew the picture existed. After the night on the roadside Amy never spoke to her angel again, but all those years later she found a picture of her and now she knows who her angel was. This was a gift from God Amy will never forget. She and Steven took the picture from the album, framed it, and have placed it over the fireplace in their home.

♥ ♥ ♥ ♥ ♥ ♥ ♥ ♥ ♥ ♥ ♥

I met Amy at a book signing one night when she was in Minnesota visiting her daughter. She and I talked for a while when she bought a copy of my book, **A Place to Warm Your Heart** *Inspirational Poems and Life Experiences*. She seemed to be a very nice lady and I would have never known about the circumstances of her life. After reading my book, she contacted me and told me her story thinking I might want to use it in a future book. I did. I too believe in angels.

We often cry out to God asking Him to help us, or sometimes to ask for something we want or think we need. All to often when we ask for things, we forget that we must have faith, and trust that God will help us. We need to believe and give Him praise, thanking Him for our many blessings.

Some of our prayers will be answered quickly, while others may take years. The truth is, even prayers that seem unanswered by God, can also be a blessing in their own way. Often we may ask for things that are not in our best interests to have, and when they are not given to us, it's for our own good. God has infinitely more wisdom than you and I, and may use these things to teach us lessons He wants us to learn. Lessons such as showing us the difference between what we want and think we need, and what He knows we need. We have to trust Jesus in these matters.

Linda C. Luebke

Have Faith

I sat quietly in the garden watching the birds play in the trees.
As they fluttered and danced against the clouds,
I felt God's love beneath their wings.

I saw the storm clouds gather, and I felt the wind upon my face.
I wondered, where do God's creatures go
When the storms begin to rage.

They have no house safe and warm to protect them through the night.
Still through the darkness and raging storm,
They're safe until mornings light.

Surely, Jesus must protect them and keep them safe from harm.
He gives them all the food they need.
In the winter He keeps them warm.

They must have faith He will do this; although, how are we to know?
They simply take a leap of faith,
And trust He won't let go.

Now, if Jesus will do these things for the sparrow in a tree,
If I'll have faith and truly believe,
What will He do for me?

Stepping out on faith, believing, I'm trusting God to lead my way.
He gives me everything I need
When, in Jesus name, I pray.

He is my shelter from life's storms. I need not fear the night.
His Spirit guides my pathway
Into heaven's gracious light.

Thank you, for your gift of love, In Jesus name I pray.
Father, please forgive my weakness.
I do believe, Lord, for I too have faith...

God will furnish our needs if we will trust him to do so. He gives us many
blessings every day. We should be grateful for these things and praise His
name, giving Him glory for all He does for us.

We all face adversities in this life. I have come to understand that how we face them can make all the difference. The human spirit is a remarkable thing. When it had been tempered with the love of God it truly knows no limit. Our Father in His infinite wisdom has given us all of the tools we will need to find our way through this life, and into heaven. If our spirit is willing, Jesus will add on the balance of what each of us may need. Thank you, Lord!

I have come to understand that at the times in my life I have called out to Jesus needing Him the most, they were probably also the times I deserved His great love the least. Still He answered with love and grace. He forgave me and made me clean. With compassion, He erased my fear and ignored my inadequacies. For this, I thank Him.

Jesus loves each of us with a love that is far beyond our comprehension. He loves us the way He would want each of us to love one another, giving nothing less than everything.

Nothing Less Than Everything

My child, so innocent, so sweet,
You depend upon me to give you everything you'd need.
There, as I held you, your life entrusted in my hands.
Because of you I've learned the power of love can rule the heart of any man.

I didn't love you half the way for you meant everything to me.
Each time you'd cried out in the night, it was my hand that you'd see.
Reaching out to brush your fear away I'd sing you back to sleep.
For love is only love when you learn to give nothing less than everything.

Throughout my life all the things I have seen
Have shown me there are many times life isn't what it seems.
And all the things that will really matter in the end,
Are things you can't put them in your pocket, or hold them in your hand.

He didn't love me half the way for I meant everything to Him.
Each time I'd cried out in the night, it was His love that He'd give.
Reaching out to brush my fear away He'd hold me through my sleep.
Teaching love is only love when you give nothing less than everything.

He can't love us half the way for that is not what His love is.
Every time we cry out in the night, He teaches us to give.
Reaching out to brush our fear away, our souls Jesus' will keep.
With love He would forgive and make me clean,
Forgiving nothing less than everything...

Linda C. Luebke

I spoke with an elderly woman one day when I was visiting a local nursing home. She expressed fear that her children would be hurt by her inability to remember things she thought she should remember. Things like their names, who married to who, the names of her grandchildren, and so on. She explained that she knew everyone, but just couldn't remember all of the details.

With a frail body and failing mind she, she fought to retain some dignity in her life. She wanted her loved one's to know how much she loved them even though the little things seemed to escape her from time to time.

Understanding that this was really bothering her, I opened the tablet of Song Poems I had with me that day, and I sang the following song to her. When I finished singing it, she reached over and touched my hand, and with tears in her eyes she smiled. In a low and fragile voice, she said, "They do understand. It's time to let them take care of me now. This is part of God's plan. They know I love them. Now it's there turn to learn compassion, just as I did when I sat with my folks at the end of their lives. I'd almost forgotten. Now I understand, this is something they need to do. Thank you for reminding me. We all need to learn these kinds of things. I feel much better now."

With Passing Time

As she sat beside the bed holding that feeble hand,
An aching heart brought tears into her eyes.
For many years it was she who depended on someone,
Who is now so weak, and it's hard to realize.

"As a child you would tell me how much I meant to you.
With all the years that passed your love has only grown.
Now I know that it's my turn to love and take care of you.
And I'll be here, always know you're not alone."

"There have been many times you don't remember who I am.
And things seem to get jumbled in your mind.
Please rest your weary heart, and find peace in this one truth,
The love you've given will last me throughout all time."

And now I pray that Jesus will gently hold your soul,
And cradle you with love eternally. I thank Him for the gift He gave
When He sent me to you with a bond of love
That will forever be."...

106

Most of us have made sacrifices in our lives, recognizing the fact that we can't have everything all of the time. I know my husband and I have done without something we wanted or need so we could give things to our children. I'm reminded of the sacrifice God made, when He sent His Son to earth that we might be forgiven and receive everlasting life.

Come, Walk With Me

Come walk with me into the past to a place we've never been.
Let's travel back to long ago when Jesus walked here among men.
Revisiting His life story may clearly help us all to see
Everything we know He is, and what we should strive to be.

With obedience, grace, and love,
He brought Faith, now that is the key.
For He came to earth to save the soul of man.
He healed the sick, He raised the dead.
The lame and blind, He let them walk and see.
With forgiveness He washed and made them clean.
He forgave the sinners, murderers, and thieves.

With five fishes and three loaves of bread, a multitude He did feed.
Upon the water He did walk, and Jesus calmed the angry sea.

He taught patience through His loving grace.
Shown us the way to live, by the example He made.
It was with kindness and with love He did all things.
And from the cross where He was crucified,
He begged His Father to forgive us, so we won't have to die.
And on a cloud He was risen back up into heaven once again.
Now from heaven He reaches out to draw us all to Him.

Into this world without a crown, this King the Son of God
Brought life and peace to all mankind, although worthy we are not.

With God's compassion and love, He gives us faith, forgiving all things...

As each of us go through this life, we will probably be faced with both many joys and much sadness. We will all have to deal with making choices, and having to live with the choices we've made. For each of us the choices we make will either make us better than we were, or sadly, much less than we might have been. All of us must make these choices for ourselves.

107

Linda C. Luebke

It is not my place to judge you, nor is it your place to judge me for the choices each of us will make. Within the souls of man, we all have the capacity to choose what we will do with our lives. We have all been given a free will and we can use it to accomplish good, or we can choose to do things most would consider less honorable. These are the choices we will make.

As we find our way down the winding, ever changing road of life we may often stumble and fall. Keep in mind as we take this journey that just because we must find our own way, it doesn't mean we have to travel alone. If we choose to ask Jesus to accompany us, He will be with us every step of the way. When we call out to Him, He will answer. I've found while on my journey through life, when I wearied and needed strength, it was Jesus who often carried me. I am forever grateful for this, and for God's unending love.

God's blessings come to us in many forms. Often we pray, asking Him to supply what we think we want and need, and then sit back and wait for a miracle. I have often wondered what it might be that God would ask of us.

I have prayed asking Jesus to heal someone on more than one occasion. In some of these cases He did heal people, but in others, He did not. Wondering why, I've searched for an answer. What I have learned if this...

We ask God to heal the body. God may choose to heal and save the soul instead, because the soul has much greater value than the body in His eyes.

We ask God to help us climb the many mountains we face in this life. Most often He allows us to find our way through these things on our own to teach us patience, tolerance, and obedience, although He is always by our side.

We ask God to give us the things that we want, thinking these things will make us happy. God gives us blessings and love. Perhaps He expects us to find happiness on our own.

We ask God to take away our pain and suffering. Sometimes he does this for us, but maybe when He doesn't, these things exist to draw us ever closer to Him, to Jesus and to the Holy Spirit.

We ask God to give us peace. He gave us His Son that we might find peace through Jesus Christ. Perhaps God would want us to seek that gift so we might learn the true value of knowing Jesus in our own lives. After all, knowing Jesus is the only way to find true peace.

We pray asking God for things we think we need, but He sees our spiritual need and recognizes this first and foremost. He also knows the difference between what we truly need and what we think we need. Perhaps he wants us to learn that lesson also.

We ask God to help us to be better than we are, so we may pass on the love He has bestowed upon us to others. Somehow, I believe this is what God would ask of each of us.

Perhaps we need to understand that when God said, "Love thy neighbor", He meant it and He was talking to you and me...

108

Now we come to the end of *A Trilogy of Hope*. As these stories unfolded I have learned several lessons from them. I understand that albeit many of the things we will face in this world may seem insurmountable at the time we are going through them, we can always find strength through Jesus, and with His help we can overcome anything.

I applaud the human spirit and its ability to overcome the adversities of this life. I recognize our spirit is a gift from God and should be treated as such. I know He will give to all of us the things we need in this life if we will ask and believe He will do so. We must have faith, hope, and patience. These are also gifts from God.

As the families depicted in this book faced the painful and horrible events detailed herein, each of them could have caved into the pressure and pain of those events and succumbed to the terror of the world. They did not. Instead, they chose to do the things that God would ask of them, and because of that choice and through the grace of Jesus, they turned their painful experiences into victories for God. The grace and courage shown by Sharon, Jenny, Amy and their families humble me.

This was difficult for each of them to do, to say the least, and it is a true testament to the love of God and to the power of the human spirit when lead by God, that each of them survived and are better for having overcome these adversities. Nothing we will face in this world has the power to pull us under if we have God in our lives. I believe these stories prove this to be true.

As I must face any problems that arise in my own life, I will remember the obstacles faced by these people, and reach out to God as they did. I hope I will be able to find a fraction of the courage they displayed.

We are all capable if doing great things in this life, if we will allow ourselves to use the many gifts God has bestowed upon us. We should use these gifts in His name, and to His glory. We are much stronger than we think we are when we have Jesus on our side. He is with us you know. We need only to call out to him. With God all things are possible, all things. We need only to ask, believe and follow.

To order additional copies of **A Place to Warm Your Heart**, complete the information below.

Ship to: (please print)

Name _____
Address_____
City, State, Zip _____

____ *A Trilogy of Hope & Inspirational Poem* @ $ 8.00 each *$*_____
____ *Inspirational Poems & Life Experiences* @ $ 8.00 each *$*_____
Postage and handling @ $ 3.00 per book *$*_____
State of MN residents add *6.5%* *$*_____
Total amount enclosed *$*_____

Make checks payable to: Linda C. Luebke

Send to: Linda C. Luebke
16019 Swallow St. NW
Andover MN 55304

To order additional copies of **A Place to Warm Your Heart**, complete the information below.

Ship to: (please print)

Name _____
Address_____
City, State, Zip _____

____ *A Trilogy of Hope & Inspirational Poem* @ $ 8.00 each *$*_____
____ *Inspirational Poems & Life Experiences* @ $ 8.00 each *$*_____
Postage and handling @ $ 3.00 per book *$*_____
State of MN residents add *6.5%* *$*_____
Total amount enclosed *$*_____

Make checks payable to: Linda C. Luebke

Send to: Linda C. Luebke
16019 Swallow St. NW
Andover MN 55304